Praise for *Words at the Threshold* by Lisa Smartt

"With *Words at the Threshold*, Lisa Smartt has given the world of near-death studies a fresh new path for research. Deeply moving and meticulously researched, this book offers a feast of fresh information about communications with the other side that may take place at the time of death. This is an insightful book worth reading."

— *Paul Perry,* coauthor of *Glimpses of Eternity*

"Rarely can we say a book has the ability to profoundly affect the way we live and think, but *Words at the Threshold* is truly such a book. The research is impeccable, and the insights that Lisa Smartt gives us into the realm of the threshold open doors of perception that help us understand what it is to be part of the human experience."

— *Michael Wayne, PhD, LAc,* author of *The Quantum Revolution* and producer and host of *Interviews with the Leading Edge*

"*Words at the Threshold* is a treasure trove of experience and insight around the last words spoken by the dying, as revealed through the mind of a linguist, proposing that birth and death are different facets of the same process, that both are essential in the cycle of life, and that our soul connections do not end with death. The words of the dying provide some of the most salient clues as to how we can best live our lives on earth."

— *Eben Alexander, MD,* neurosurgeon and author of *Proof of Heaven* and *The Map of Heaven*

"*Words at the Threshold* marks a new era in the understanding of the process of dying. Lisa Smartt's work has profound psychological, spiritual, and clinical implications for the care of terminally ill patients and their families. And I believe that her work also opens unexplored pathways for the genuinely rational investigation of humankind's deepest mystery: the prospect of life after death."

— from the foreword by *Raymond Moody Jr., MD, PhD,* author of *Life After Life*

"Lisa Smartt gently invites us to listen to the utterances of the dying with an inner ear attuned to another kind of reality. She charts how the dying use eerily familiar metaphors, symbols, time loops, and more to express their expanded, nonlinear experiences. In so doing, Smartt affords us a precious glimpse of their inner worlds as they linger at the threshold of death. Through her linguistic analysis of 'nonsense' on the lips of the dying, the underlying creativity and purpose of final words are revealed. *Words at the Threshold* is a significant step toward transforming the current views of dying from a process of failure into a process of ever-deepening meaning and wonder."

— *Julia Assante, PhD,* author of *The Last Frontier*

WORDS
at the
THRESHOLD

My Dearest
Claire —

Thank you for
your very beautiful
work bedside —
you are kindred,
indeed — love
Lisa Smartt

WORDS
at the
THRESHOLD

WHAT WE SAY
AS WE'RE
NEARING DEATH

LISA SMARTT

Foreword by Raymond Moody Jr., MD, PhD

New World Library
Novato, California

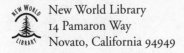

New World Library
14 Pamaron Way
Novato, California 94949

The material in this book is intended for education. Some names have been changed to protect the privacy of individuals.

Text design by Tracy Cunningham

Library of Congress Cataloging-in-Publication Data
Names: Smartt, Lisa, author.
Title: Words at the threshold : what we say as we're nearing death / Lisa
    Smartt ; foreword by Raymond Moody, Jr., MD, PhD.
Description: Novato, California : New World Library, [2017] | Includes
    bibliographical references and index.
Identifiers: LCCN 2016046063 (print) | LCCN 2017003617 (ebook) | ISBN
    9781608684601 (alk. paper) | ISBN 9781608684618 (Ebook)
Subjects: LCSH: Near-death experiences. | Last words. | Death. | Future life.
Classification: LCC BF1045.N4 S63 2017 (print) | LCC BF1045.N4 (ebook)
    | DDC
    133.901/3—dc23
LC record available at https://lccn.loc.gov/2016046063

First printing, March 2017
ISBN 978-1-60868-460-1
Ebook ISBN 978-1-60868-461-8

Printed in Canada on 100% postconsumer-waste recycled paper

 New World Library is proud to be a Gold Certified Environmentally Responsible Publisher. Publisher certification awarded by Green Press Initiative. www.greenpressinitiative.org

10   9   8   7   6   5   4   3   2   1

*For my father, who continues to sing to me
in "an octave higher than grief"*

Contents

Foreword

W*ords at the Threshold* marks a new era in the understanding of
the process of dying. Lisa Smartt's work has profound psychological, spiritual, and clinical implications for the care of terminally ill patients and their families. And I believe that her work also
opens unexplored pathways for the genuinely rational investigation
of humankind's deepest mystery: the prospect of life after death.

My main interest as a student and subsequently professor of
philosophy had to do with the fascinating domains of language that
exist beyond the literal. I studied figurative and unintelligible or
nonsensical forms of language for their relevance to the solutions
of important philosophical problems. Later on, as a medical doctor
and psychiatrist, I was intrigued by the enigmatic language spoken
by terminally ill and dying patients. Like many other clinicians, I
was inspired and mystified by curious figures of speech and nonsensical expressions that people often utter as they are dying. In
fact, the unintelligible language of dying patients is sometimes as
eloquent as the nonsense of the great literary artists such as Lewis
Carroll.

In shamanism, ancient magic, and the Western literary tradition, nonsense once signified the transition from this world to other dimensions of existence. I have long contended that the structure of nonsense holds the key to rational comprehension of the mysteries of the afterlife. A major rethinking of the meaning of puzzling language spoken by the terminally ill is long overdue. Lisa Smartt's captivating analysis of this phenomenon will be the starting point of many future doctoral dissertations and clinical studies. Her trailblazing book will also comfort and enlighten many who have marveled at the enigmatic final words of their departed loved ones.

— Raymond Moody Jr., MD, PhD, author of *Life After Life*

Words at the Threshold

What Our Final Conversations Tell Us

One day, if not today, you will sit at the bedside of someone you love and have a final conversation. That conversation will invite you into a unique territory — the one that exists between living and dying. You may hear words expressing a desire for forgiveness, reconciliation, or the fulfillment of last requests. You may hear phrases that confuse you, like "The circles say it's time to complete the cycle."

There may be references to things you do not see or understand, such as "The white butterflies are coming out of your mouth. They are beautiful." Or "If you have passed the quiz. You have passed the quiz, haven't you?"

Your beloved may describe being visited by deceased family members, angels, or animals or speak of viewing lush landscapes, where in reality there are only white hospital walls. Trains, boats, or buses and tales of new travels may appear in the speech of the person who is dying. Your family member or friend may also speak of being afraid and seek your comfort as well as your guidance:

"I am stuck here between two countries. I am here but I want to be there." Your beloved may whisper in your ear, "Help me," or, "I am daring to die."

And as you listen closely, it may be a conversation that changes not only how you think about dying but also how you think about living.

Words at the Threshold is an investigation into the remarkable things people say at the end of life. Over a period of four years, I collected accounts and transcripts from health-care providers, friends, and family members of the dying who generously shared what they had witnessed. Through the Final Words Project, its website, Facebook, and email, I gathered data across the United States and Canada while also conducting interviews in person and by phone. I gathered over fifteen hundred English utterances, which ranged from single words to complete sentences, from those who were a few hours to a few weeks from dying.

While I considered the use of digital recorders at the bedsides of the dying to capture final utterances, the sacred and private nature of those last days made this both ethically and logistically untenable. So, I decided to turn to those who had been at the bedside — loved ones and health-care providers — and ask them to share transcriptions, interviews, and recollections. I also interviewed professionals in the fields of linguistics, psychology, palliative medicine, and neuroscience to gain greater insight into terminal illness and cognitive and psychological processes. Participants included the dying individuals I heard or observed directly, family members and friends who shared transcriptions and accounts, and experts in the field who shared their observations.

I organized the language samples and accounts by linguistic features and themes. Many of the patterns that emerged were present also in the observations of health-care professionals and experts I interviewed. As I learned of these patterns, I shared them with families, friends, and hospice personnel with the aim of offering tools and insight that could guide their communications with the dying. I am not a medical expert — my training is in linguistics — so I approach the study of death and dying through the lens of language.

This inquiry was inspired by what I heard and saw in the three weeks my father spent dying from complications related to radiation therapy for prostate cancer. As I sat with him, it was as if a portal had opened — and I discovered a new language, one rich with metaphor and nonsense that spilled from my father's lips. As I transcribed his words from between the worlds, I witnessed a remarkable transformation.

My father was a cigar-chomping New Yorker whose definition of the Divine was corned beef on rye with slaw on the side and a cold glass of cream soda. He placed his faith in Lucky Sam in the fifth race and in his beloved wife of fifty-four years, Susan. "This is it," my dad would say when asked about his spiritual life. "Good food, love, and the ponies." My father savored life's pleasures and was both a skeptic and a rationalist. "We are all headed for the same afterlife, six feet under."

So when he started talking about seeing and hearing angels in his last weeks of life, I was stunned. How was it that my father, a skeptic, would accurately predict the timing of his own death with these words: "Enough...enough...the angels say enough... only three days left..."? From the moment he left the hospital after deciding to come home to die, I was struck by his language. Compelled by my linguistics training, I grabbed pencil and paper and tracked his final utterances as if I were a visitor in a foreign country. For indeed, I was.

Words at the Threshold documents my research into this new territory. This inquiry began with my father's language and, within four years, became a collection of hundreds of utterances analyzed for their linguistic patterns and themes. The words I collected were much like my father's: sometimes confusing, often metaphoric, frequently nonsensical, and always intriguing. I have come to understand that the language patterns and themes that at first stunned me in my father's speech are actually common in the speech of others as they approach the end of life.

The First Final Words

The first example of this form of speech occurred when my father's speaking initially began to shift — less than a month before his very unexpected death. On a January night, my father walked out the front door wearing only his underwear and strolled down a busy avenue. When the police found him sitting at an intersection, trembling with cold, he explained, "Tonight is the big exhibition, and I am bringing boxes to my wife's art gallery for the show. Do you know where the big exhibition is going to be?" They helped my father up from the curb and shook their heads with pity as they led the seventy-seven-year-old to an ambulance. There were no boxes in his hands. There was no art exhibition.

The big exhibition my father talked about was merely an analogy — and I would soon discover that this kind of analogy was common as people neared death. He was telling those who listened to him, as he spoke a language veiled in the symbol of the art show, that a major occurrence would soon take place. For over five decades, my father schlepped boxes to my mother's art galleries and exhibitions. Carrying boxes for her was in his blood, his cells; it was one of the metaphors of his lifetime. He used an analogy connected closely to his life, as the dying often do, to announce his death.

Using the symbols of the big art show, he was letting us know: pay attention, because something major is happening. He was getting ready to die. But at the time, none of us knew that this kind of figurative language is common in the words of the dying. We dismissed my father's utterances as mere "word salad" or the result of medications he had begun taking. However, I would find out later that they were neither.

After my father passed away, I had a notebook filled with utterances that captivated and confused me. My father spoke of travels to Las Vegas, of the green dimension, of his room crowded with people unseen to me. He used repetition frequently, as well as non-referential pronouns such as the ones in these sentences: "*This* is very interesting. You know, I've never done *this* before." On my notebook pages were metaphors and nonsense, remarks so different from the lucid language that was typical of my father when he was healthy. As I looked through the pages, I noticed how the phrases reflected a full continuum from literal to figurative to nonsensical language — and I wondered if this continuum was common to us all and in any way tracked the path of consciousness as we die.

In the days and weeks when I was grieving, I read every book I could find about communication at the end of life and after life. Little has been written about the qualities of and change in the structure of end-of-life language, though I did find a wonderful book, *Final Gifts*, by Maggie Callanan and Patricia Kelley. Even when I searched the linguistics databases at my alma mater, University of California, Berkeley, I found little about the language of the dying.

Raymond Moody and the Final Words Project

At this time, I decided to unearth a book that had intrigued me when I was sixteen years old: *Life After Life*, by Raymond Moody, in which he coined the term *near-death experience*. I was rereading the book when my mother told me that a friend had just shared the exciting news that in a few weeks he would be teaching a class with Dr. Moody in Alabama. "Maybe you could go and meet him!" my mother said. "I know you have so many questions."

The workshop took place in a large stone-and-wood lodge in the Alabama hills. There were fifteen of us from all around the country who joined together to learn from Raymond Moody. His book had completely changed the conversation about death and dying back in 1975, when it was published. Yet despite the millions of books sold and thousands of public appearances, the person who sat before us was an unpretentious and gentle man who sipped Diet Cokes and wore tennis shoes as he shared his wisdom of four decades spent researching death, grief, and the afterlife. His spirit of inquiry deeply moved me. And then, on the fourth day of the workshop, he shared excerpts from his unpublished manuscript "Making Sense of Nonsense," which reflected forty years of investigation into language. After I returned home, he sent me a copy and I read every page closely. Days later, I announced to my husband and daughter: "I have to study with this man."

Words at the Threshold shares the discoveries I made during the years I spent working with Raymond Moody and establishing the Final Words Project.

The Nature of This Inquiry

This investigation is not formal or rigorous. That is, it does not control for medications or illness. I offer a detailed explanation — informed by hospice professionals, palliative-care researchers, and the data itself — of why controlling for medications may not be necessary in order to find valid information as we study final words. The same patterns seem to emerge whether someone is highly medicated or not medicated at all; this is also true of the patterns associated with near-death experiences.

Moreover, because we are sense-making creatures, unintelligible language is often not noticed, or is completely discounted, by those who hear it. While I asked participants to transcribe or recall puzzling and nonsensical phrases, I suspect that there was language overlooked because it was meaningless to family members and health-care providers. An important part of this book focuses on unintelligible language and its emergence at the end of life, and I acknowledge that the discussion of unintelligibility presented here is likely incomplete; however, even so, enough similarities and patterns emerge in the data that this study qualifies as a first step in this inquiry.

Finally, those who shared their stories with me very likely were moved to chronicle and share transpersonal or positive experiences, since it is much more difficult to speak about frightening or difficult ones. For this reason, the results may be skewed in favor of more positive accounts. And yet, even with these limitations, the findings gleaned from this research offer insights into the questions that first inspired this investigation: Do consistent patterns emerge in the language of the end of life? And if so, what exactly are those patterns and how might they track the path of consciousness?

From my interviews with friends, family members, health-care providers, and researchers, it appears that in hospitals, homes, and hospices, the dying enter new states of being, and their words are a window into those states. My research of four years indicates that my father was not alone in experiencing metaphorical and nonsensical changes in language, seeing visions of angels, and making references to another dimension in his final days.

In the chapters ahead, I share with you the compelling language I have heard and the coherency that emerges in even the most puzzling phrases. The words at the threshold suggest to me that consciousness does indeed survive, and that we ourselves can be both guides and tourists as we journey with those we love to the portal.

CHAPTER ONE

Transcribing the Mystery
Following the Sacred Path of Final Words

There is so much so in sorrow.
— *My father's final words*

Imagine you have reached the end of your life. Your beloveds stand at your bedside. You look into their eyes and prepare to speak. It is a moment to heal wounds, express love unsaid, and share your view from the threshold. It is a sacred time, when all of life is concentrated into those final breath-filled syllables.

What do you see?

What do you feel?

What are your final words?

Very little has been written about final words other than what is found in anthologies and websites that quote the clever exit lines of the famous. They include accounts of conversations like that of comedian Bob Hope with his wife, who, alarmed by her husband's rapid decline, told him: "Bob, we never made arrangements for your burial. Where do you want to be buried, honey? We have to figure this out. Where do you want to be buried?"

His response, typical of his dry wit: "Surprise me!"

As is often the case with last words, Hope's were true to character.

The awe-filled exclamation of Apple's Steve Jobs — "Oh, wow! Oh, wow! Oh, wow!" — is an example of the intensified language we hear at the threshold and is true to the personality of the inspired innovator. Another well-known pioneer, Thomas Edison, emerged from a coma as he was dying, opened his eyes, looked upward, and said, "It is very beautiful over there." As you will see, his words were representative of those of others who have stared out from the threshold. Many other final words have been chronicled, from Karl Marx's "Go on, get out! Last words are for fools who haven't said enough!" to Emily Dickinson's "I must go in, for the fog is rising."

Chaz Ebert, wife of celebrity critic Roger Ebert, shared a detailed account of her husband's last words, in *Esquire* in 2013:

> That week before Roger passed away, I would see him and he would talk about having visited this other place. I thought he was hallucinating. I thought they were giving him too much medication. But the day before he passed away, he wrote me a note: "This is all an elaborate hoax." I asked him, "What's a hoax?" And he was talking about this world, this place. He said it was all an illusion. I thought he was just confused. But he was not confused. He wasn't visiting heaven, not the way we think of heaven. He described it as a vastness that you can't even imagine. It was a place where the past, present, and future were happening all at once.

These remarkable words were read with fascination by people throughout the country — and have the authentic complexity of the words I have heard at the bedsides of those I have researched. However, the authenticity of less contemporaneous reports of the last words of famous figures is at times questionable. Ray Robinson, who compiled *Famous Last Words, Fond Farewells,*

Deathbed Diatribes, and Exclamations upon Expiration, notes in the introduction to his book: "I've come to appreciate the difficulty of authenticating so-called exit lines, since witnesses are often too distraught or confused to remember things accurately, or simply choose to edit or improve the remarks for the sake of posterity."

However, for the rest of us who are not celebrities, our last words go unedited and unrecorded in time. And yet all of us are given a platform before dying. Every day, compelling last words are spoken — and they are rarely as simple or clever as what we might find between the covers of books and magazines. Many final words are less literal, less intelligible, and more enigmatic — and their complexity makes them even more remarkable.

Sanctified Language at the End of Life

Our final words deeply reflect who we are and what most matters to us. It is as if the lens of our Creator is magnified and all that we are is in close view. As I discuss in later chapters, even those who have been in a coma and those who have not communicated in years may speak just before they die, to advise, forgive, love, or even to leave friends and family with mysterious phrases, such as "It's not that," "The pronoun is all wrong," "I left the money in the third drawer down," or a simple "Thank you. I love you."

Buddhists believe that reflecting upon what might be our last words can deepen our acceptance of life's impermanence and remind us to savor the present moment. In Buddhist and Hindu belief systems it has been a tradition for the dying to offer parting words of wisdom. Some Buddhist monks have even composed poems in their final moments. Those who are dying are often perceived as having access to truths and revelations not available to those who are living. In anthologies of days gone by, deathbed conversions were documented, and final words acted as testaments to an almighty God and the existence of angels. End-of-life confessions offered people a chance to repent sins and beg forgiveness. Final words are still considered a golden seal upon our lives, like a stamp that sums up all our deeds and days and lets those around us know what we believe in and what really matters.

Those who are on their deathbeds seem to have a kind of privileged connection to God, or Source, or all of creation. Some might ask, "Why do we assume final words to be somehow closer to God's truth?" And that is a good question. A large amount of literature answers this in spiritual terms: when we approach death, we are returning to Source, and our thoughts and words are therefore elevated because of this shift in dimension. The findings of the Final Words Project suggest that this may, indeed, be true.

Among those I interviewed for the book is the Reverend Cari Rush Willis, a chaplain who works on death row and in a hospice. She shared her perspective about the enigmatic words we hear from the dying: "People at the end of their lives have one foot in heaven and one foot on earth." She shared an example of a care-home director who asked for her help because one of the Alzheimer's patients kept requesting assistance in finding his passport. Willis explained to the director that the patient did not have a physical problem that needed to be solved but a spiritual one that needed to be heard. She repeated to me her conversation with the dying man:

"You lost your passport. That sounds very upsetting."

"Yes, yes, it is. I cannot go where I need to."

"Oh, wow. You cannot go. You are stuck."

"Yes, I am stuck here between two countries. I am here but I want to be there."

"Oh, you want to be there."

"Yes, I so long to be there."

"Yes, yes, you so long to be there."

He calmed down considerably and said, "Yes, I long to be there."

In the accounts of the dying, many "long to be there," and the journey of "arriving peacefully" is revealed in remarkable language, which we will see in the chapters ahead.

Asking the Big Questions

I asked clergy and hospice workers to tell me the most commonly asked questions at the end of life. All of them said the one they hear most often is "What if there really is no heaven or God?" Here are some of the others they said they commonly hear:

> What's going to happen to me in the days ahead?
> What's going to happen after I die?
> Is there really a God?
> Will I be going to heaven?

Reverend Willis counsels that no matter who we are or how we lived, we should be given the opportunity to ask the big questions and find our own answers. Most of the experts I interviewed agreed. Counselor and death educator Martha Jo Atkins suggested responding to people's questions about God with another question, such as "What is God to you?" and then guiding them to their own answers.

"I ask: what and how do you picture heaven to be?" retired hospice nurse and social worker Kathy Notarino told me. "I would never try to change that belief for them. If they ask me what I believe, I say I know there is life beyond this physical world, but that I have a hard time really knowing what it looks like."

We, of course, hope for ourselves and those we love that at the moment of crossing we will be filled with awe like Jobs or Edison, or that our experience will be like that of one dying inmate who was comforted in his final days by Reverend Willis. She described how this emotionally calloused and crusty old inmate had a profound moment of revelation in her presence.

> One of the first people I sat with was an ornery old Texan. He was sitting in the corner of his cell — I could see him looking up at the corner, as I later found out many people do as they die. It was as if the heavens had opened up and he could see something broad and vast. His eyes grew large and his old countenance changed. He looked up at the ceiling of his cell and stammered out, "God is…greater… greater than anything I could ever hope for or imagine," as big tears flowed down his face. I swear he was looking at heaven when he said it!

"Am I going to heaven? Is there really a God?" For some at the threshold, these big questions are never answered. Writer Gertrude Stein asked on her deathbed: "What is the answer?" When no answer came to her, she laughed and said, "In that case what is the question?" Soon after, she died. Her words, like those of Roger Ebert (and others in their final days), seem to indicate a kind of absurd understanding of what happens as they cross the threshold. In death, as in life, we formulate our own questions and find our own answers.

Health-care providers told me that many people — even those who have anxiety and discomfort in the dying process — often have a breakthrough. This breakthrough is often associated with bedside visions, healing dreams, conversations with both living and deceased beloveds, or other exceptional experiences. We can track these remarkable experiences through the shifts in language, discussed in later chapters. The breakthroughs often result in greater ease, surrender, relaxation — even awe — as people die.

Anna Rosen, a hospice nurse, told me:

There is a difference between the dying and the ill — and you can see it in their eyes. When people are ill and have a high temperature, they may see things, and there is often an underlying fear because they don't understand. Whereas with the end-of-life experiences, it is like a process, a process that takes people to a different level. End-of-life experiences are often positive for people. The things they see, the changes they go through: it is like a journey.

However, clearly not everyone journeys gently into that good night, and some die having never made peace or having fully resolved the life issues that allow for tranquil transitions.

Kathy Notarino shared the following with me: "In my experience, many people die as they lived. If they were always in control and had difficulty showing emotions to family and friends, then they seem to struggle more. Many have unresolved issues with their partners or children, even their life. They fight like hell to give up losing their lives and very seldom have the deathbed visions that often bring relief and comfort."

These deathbed visions Kathy referred to often occur as people are very close to dying and usually involve deceased friends and family who come to "take the person away." Chapter 7 focuses on this well-documented phenomenon — and its powerfully comforting effect. However, not everyone experiences the reassurance that comes with deathbed "visitations."

Tai chi and meditation teacher Jeffrey Kessler described his father's last days as his body weakened with an accelerating heart condition. Jeffrey explained, "He was the kind of person who fought any kind of vulnerability." Jeffrey's father was a World War II veteran and had always wanted to teach his "too-soft son" to be tough.

More than once, his father had quoted these lines from "Invictus," by William Ernest Henley: "I am the master of my fate; I am the captain of my soul."

After a catastrophic heart attack, followed by a week of treatments with no improvement, his father, in the hours before dawn, asked the nurses to pull the plug. They did and then called Jeffrey and his two brothers to let them know their father would soon be dying. As they gathered at their father's side, he somehow managed to hoist himself up to a sitting position in bed and quoted the words Jeffrey had come to know so well: "I am the master of my fate; I am the captain of my soul" — and then his dad yelled "Bullshit!" and died.

Jeffrey explained to me, "He liked to think of himself as a powerful padrone, but before death he was physically humbled. And as the fortress of his heart crumbled, he felt his complete powerlessness in the face of the big mystery."

Each of us undertakes the process of facing the mystery differently. When my father was dying and we would inquire how he was doing, he would answer, "I am working on myself, working on myself." This was a phrase he used throughout life when he tried to find ways to deal with challenging people or circumstances. My family members all felt there was great truth in what he told us. Even in the end, he was working toward a deeper understanding of his process and of his life.

Final Requests

One of the ways people bring closure to their lives is through their final requests. The most common requests in the Final Words Project were humble ones related to visiting with friends and family members and enjoying certain small pleasures, like a last bottle of a favorite beer. Those who are dying often wait for certain friends or relatives so they can say good-bye. Final requests often take the form of ensuring that those they love will have all they need to continue forward. A typical example was a man's advice to his daughter to make sure that his granddaughter "gets lots of guitar lessons." To that, he added, "She is very talented, you know." Another father told his son, "I am worried about your mother. She doesn't seem well."

One son described how his mother emerged from a completely unresponsive state a couple of days before dying to inform him about the location of important financial files that would settle her estate — making everything easier for him.

One patient requested the quilt that had warmed her many nights as she sat beside the woodstove of her mountain cabin; she sought its familiar comfort hours before dying.

My grandmother asked to have chocolate shavings placed on her tongue.

On Thanksgiving Day, the father of a large family, Steven Ross, asked that the carving tools for the Thanksgiving turkey be brought to his hospital bed so he could serve his favorite meal to those he loved. His family lovingly brought some turkey and a dull knife to him. Only partly lucid, he imagined it was an earlier time, and he encouraged all to enjoy the season's bounty.

Rachel Weintraub described how her sister, who was dying of lung cancer, wanted a cigarette and pancakes before dying. The nurse, not honoring the woman's last request, upped her morphine dosage — with disastrous effects. "My sister did not get either of her requests," Rachel wrote. "Not a happy ending."

Hopefully, you and your loved one will be in a place where last requests are fully honored — whether chocolate or a cigarette, a visit from a certain son or uncle, or pancakes heaped with syrup and whipped cream. For my dad it was the chance to choose one more winner at the horse races, which he got to watch on television, and the opportunity to admire, on video, his silver-screen goddess

Marilyn Monroe one last time while she sang, "A kiss on the hand may be quite continental..."

Stepping into Another World

Developing a rapport with someone, or stepping into that person's world, is the most powerful way to build a connection. In the early 1970s, John Grinder, an assistant professor of linguistics at the University of California, Santa Cruz, and Richard Bandler, a student of psychology, identified patterns used by successful therapists. One fruitful strategy among the therapists was to match the lead representational system of the client. Each of us processes our experiences and represents them to ourselves and others differently — and these are revealed in visual, auditory, or kinesthetic terms.

Bandler and Grinder discovered that when a client speaks in visual terms, saying, for example, "I just can't *see* what I am doing wrong," the most effective therapists consciously or unconsciously match the modality of the person speaking and say something like "Let's take a *look* and *focus* more closely on this." Or, when clients would say something like "I just can't *grasp* why it is not working out," the therapists would use kinesthetic phrasing in reply, such as "I *get* what you mean...I *feel* you."

When people feel that you are meeting them where they are, they feel "seen," "heard," or "known" and are comforted by that. Any act of communication offers an opportunity for building a bridge. One of the ways to do this is to listen to the language of the other person and match it. In this way you enter into the speaker's reality and validate it. When you do this, it opens doors in multiple ways and allows for a deepening of rapport.

The week when my father began dying, he sat up in bed, looked at me with his piercing eyes, and said, "What the hell is going on? Am I dying?" I was so terrified of this question that I never answered him. How does a daughter tell her father he is dying — especially as she faces her own fear and grief? So, unprepared for his inquiry, I was not able to fully enter into the reality of the moment. I did not know then how to comfortably and fully step into his world.

I sought the advice of my friend Barbara, who is a therapist. I asked how I should answer my father if he ever asked me again. She said, "Most people do know when they're dying. Instead of being frightened to be honest, be honest. The dying are usually so lonely, since everyone is avoiding the truth. Don't worry — you can't kill a dying person by admitting he might be dying. It's no shock to him. Be honest about the reality of dying, and then the two of you can get real about your feelings."

In some families, confronting this reality comes more easily. I interviewed Jerry, a middle-aged businessman, who shared a story with me about his aunt, Francine. She had no trouble speaking directly about death. Francine had left hospice care, opting to die at home, and was resting in the bedroom. Jerry explained that the whole family, who had come from different parts of the country to be with the aunt, had gathered in the dining room to eat and had begun to talk loudly together, as was customary during their meals. The aunt in the other room cried out, "Can you all quiet down, please. I am fucking trying to die in here!"

One father told his daughter as he was nearing death: "I am daring to die." His was a truth that she could hear, but not all people can fully articulate or confront death with such clear courage. In my interviews with families, I found that they had different ways of speaking about death. Some were direct, in many cases because an early diagnosis had opened the doors to communication for them. In other families, there was little or no candid conversation between the dying and their beloveds.

"What to say to a loved one who asks, 'Am I going to die?'" hospice nurse Kathy Notarino remarked in response to my email inquiry. She went on to say, "That is a hard one, because it really depends on the people and how they will take that info. I took care of my mom, who asked [that question]. When she was having a good day, I would say, 'Not today.' I also said, 'I don't know,' but I think she knew. It is hard with a parent. I just took care of my good friend, who died of ovarian cancer, and we talked openly about it because she knew I would tell her the truth."

In my case, I never honestly and directly answered my father's question, and yes, as Barbara suggested, I felt that he knew. While he and I never fully connected in response to his question, we fell into rapport in the weeks afterward. There are many ways and opportunities to connect with our beloveds in the final days and weeks of life, and they may not all be literal conversations. There are touch points in every phase before the person we love leaves us, and this book is, in part, about learning those touch points and trusting in the sacred openings that exist at each one.

By the time I thought I had an answer that would allow my father and me to speak literally and honestly about his dying, it was too late to have the conversation. He was already traveling on, moving into a world where his words were harder to understand and where he began to speak in symbolic, cryptic language. The question of whether he was dying no longer hung in the air. He had entered a new state of being, one that allowed him to make peace with the reality he had begun to fully confront.

If Someone You Love Is Dying Now

If you are facing the death of a beloved right now, I invite you to write down the words you hear — even those that seem to make no sense — without editing, fearing, or judging them. As you transcribe the words, and as you read through these chapters, you may discover that the very changes you hear in your beloved's language, which may seem scary and confusing, may ultimately bring you comfort and meaning.

Jewels often emerge as we listen closely and write down final words, and the transcription process can help us feel more connected to our loved ones and even closer to Source. Many times the dying say things that don't make sense at the moment. But months or years later, you will find hints of prophecy or answers to questions in those words.

Here are some suggestions for you to use as you courageously and compassionately witness final words.

— *Enter the world of your beloved.* Imagine you are visiting a new country. Keep an open heart and mind. Record in a final-words journal what you hear, see, and feel; it will be your private travelogue about that other place. You may be surprised later by the pearls of wisdom you find there.

— *Have eyes for the sacred.* If possible, imagine that the territory you have entered is sacred ground, despite the terrible loss looming before you. Be open to the possibility that something transpersonal is occurring, and that the words you hear are tracking its course.

— *Validate your loved one's words and experiences.* Repeat back what your beloved has said, to let the person know you heard it: "Oh, your modality is broken. I would love to know more about that." Avoid telling your beloved that what he or she is seeing or saying is wrong or "not real."

— *Be a student of the language.* Since you are in a new country, learn its language. Study it. Practice it. Speak it. Listen for the symbols and metaphors that are meaningful to your beloved and then use them when you communicate. For example, ask, "Would you like me to help you find your passport?" When you hear things that sound nonsensical, simply think, "Oh, that's how they phrase things in *this* country!"

— *Ask questions with authenticity and curiosity.* It's okay to let the dying person know you are confused and would love to hear more of what he or she wants to communicate. "Could you tell me more about…?"

— *Assume your loved one can hear you even when unresponsive or quiet; let the dying person know how deep your love goes.* As we die, our sense of hearing is the last sense to go. When you are in another room, and especially when you are speaking about your beloved, speak with lots of praise and gratitude. Speak words that will bring joy or comfort to the person.

— *Savor silence.* Sometimes it is better to just sit with your loved one. When words don't build bridges, know that the dying may be much more attuned to telepathic or other nonverbal communication, much like the kind of communication we experience when we pray. Speak to the person you love as you would in prayer.

Healing Grief

Your listening to and honoring final words will make the dying process easier for your beloved. At the same time, transcribing the words can be healing for you as you move through the loss of someone you love. Make a journal out of the words you're writing down. Remember that the words that don't make sense are as important as the ones that do. Notice metaphors or symbols that are repeated, and paradoxical phrases. Are there certain colors or shapes that are repeated? Are there references to people or places you do not see? Meanings may not be clear at first, but when you write down the words you have heard, you may find comforting or healing associations.

What might seem senseless to a stranger may hold deep personal meaning to you. Final words can be like dreams. We learn so much by reflecting upon these words and free-associating with them. In your final-words journal, write down the words you hear, and allow yourself to free-associate. Imagine the words are those of an oracle, or the wisdom of dreams, and let them evoke images and reflections in you. You may be surprised and moved by what emerges.

My mother and I created raku-fired plaques of my father's final words in honor of his memory. Art is a powerful healing tool. Many times, the best way to process grief is without language. Taking final words and building art with them and through them brings us to a greater understanding of their meaning and of those we love. Integrating final words with art is one way to keep the portal open between the living and the dying, and a way to honor those who left before us.

Shedding Light on the Path of Consciousness

If you are not currently facing the loss of someone you love, it is my hope that this book will offer you the tools for when you do. Perhaps it will also answer your questions about an afterlife and deepen your appreciation of the connection between language and consciousness.

As much as the death of a beloved is grief-filled, it is often also a sacred time. The language at the end of life offers a pathway to a better understanding of the spiritual quality of dying and living — and can help us develop deeper connections with our beloveds. With each word we transcribe, we are invited into the consciousness of those we care about as they transition.

The continuum of language in the communications of the dying includes an increase in symbolic and metaphoric language, repetition, sustained narratives, various kinds of paradoxical and situational "nonsense," and a variety of other linguistic patterns that shed light on the path of consciousness that we traverse as we die. By analyzing the language of those who have had near-death experiences, we can learn from these accounts about words at the threshold.

CHAPTER TWO

No Words for It

Language Changes as We Approach the Threshold

I cannot put words to the experience.
There is no way I could ever fully explain it.
— *Sandra, Final Words Project participant*

Y ou are describing to a friend what a chair looks like. That's simple, isn't it?

How about explaining the sensation of being in love?

Can you easily convey the taste of a chocolate bar to someone who has never eaten chocolate?

Now, how would you describe a deeply spiritual moment to someone who has never had one?

Certain concepts are harder to put into words than others. If you are like most people, you will find the task of describing a chair to be relatively easy. You will use literal and intelligible language: for example, you might say it has four legs that are made of oak, a hard back, and a cushioned seat made of blue velvet. That's easy enough. And the person you are speaking to will likely understand everything you are saying — there is little chance for misunderstanding. Your two perceptions of reality in this case overlap pretty closely.

Language can range from highly literal to figurative to unintelligible. While most human speech is literal or figurative, unintelligible or "nonsense" language sometimes occurs. We often use figurative language and even nonsensical language when we describe things that are difficult to express in literal language.

Let's go back to explaining the sensation of being in love. Suddenly you might need to resort to language beyond the literal to explain it. You might say something like "The moment I met him, I felt as if I had known him for a million years." Or "When we are together, I feel a peace I have never known before — like being in the mountains under a starry sky."

Since we are not very accustomed to describing tastes, and in English we have a relatively narrow vocabulary for talking about flavors, conversations about chocolate might be even more difficult than those about love. You might have to make comparisons and associations. "It tastes sweet and rich and creamy. Kind of a dark flavor...makes me think of wild jungles — but with all the sweetness of fruit. And there is something almost soothing about it as it melts on the tongue..."

And finally, if you have an extremely spiritual experience, there may be an even narrower band of language you can use to share this intensely subjective experience with another person. We have so few literal phrases that can describe intensely internal moments. That is why poets and mystics often turn to figurative and even nonsensical language to talk about things in life that are not sensory. It is not unusual for nonsensory mystical experience to be explored through non-*sense*-ical paradoxes such as "the whispering silence" or "the illuminated darkness."

Literal language works well for those things that involve the five senses and are shared by all of us. However, when the experiences or concepts are more subjective and move beyond the purely sensory, finding the right words becomes increasingly difficult.

How to Describe the Experience of Dying?

So imagine for a moment: What kind of language might you use to describe the experience of dying?

Not only is it an experience for which the listener has no compelling reference point, but also it is completely strange and new to the person who is dying. It is, in every way, completely without a frame of reference for most of us. Consider, as well, both the possibility that dying is an incomprehensible *this*, as my father described it to his secretary a few days before dying ("*This* is very interesting, Alice"), and the possibility that if there is another dimension or an afterlife, it too would elude all the literal meanings we have known in this world. Perhaps just by crossing into these new dimensions, we engage new parts of our brains and, as a result, our language.

Those who have had near-death experiences say it is impossible to find the words to explain their experience. Their experience is *ineffable*.

When we look at the continuum of language from literal to nonsensical, something fascinating emerges: These different kinds of language are associated with different parts of the brain, according to recent brain-scan research. Literal language, the kind you use to describe a chair, engages regions in the left hemisphere, which have traditionally been associated with the language of literal, shared reality. But figurative language, such as the simile "My love is like a red, red rose," engages both the left and right hemispheres in the brain. In an article published in *Scientific American* the author explains, "Previous brain-imaging research has shown that interpreting metaphors requires a variety of areas on both sides of the brain, compared with literal language, which is processed in known language areas in the left hemisphere." However, a nonsense sentence, such as "My love is thorning the spiraling plotz," engages the right hemisphere's regions associated with mystical experiences and music, as we will see later in much greater detail.

Is it possible, then, that as we approach death we have experiences that are more difficult to express with the usual range of language, so there is an increase in metaphoric and puzzling constructions? Or is it that as we die, regions of the left hemisphere associated with literal, sensory language become degraded? And that, as a result, there is greater reliance on language that involves right-hemispheric functions in those days before death? Or are both ideas true? Are we wired to have experiences at the end of life that fall outside of literal language, and do these experiences have the effect of somehow arresting or interfering with our left-hemispheric functions, so that degradation of the literal-language functions leads to more symbolic and non-sense-ical experiences?

Raymond Moody suggests that when "the mind shifts from an intelligible dimension to a less comprehensible dimension, it generates nonsense; a literal account would just be wrong. The mind is forced to talk nonsense transitioning between dimensions." Moody uses the word *nonsense* to refer to language that does not make literal sense to those who hear it. However, he also indicates that almost every language is unintelligible "nonsense" to those who do not know the language and its spoken and written linguistic patterns: for example, Chinese is nonsense to those who do not speak it. As we learn more about the continuum of language that appears in our final days, it becomes increasingly meaningful to us and sounds less like nonsense.

The Language of the Near-Death Experience

Raymond Moody's understanding of the unique properties of unintelligible language was, in part, what led him to coin the term *near-death experience*. Before becoming a medical doctor, he earned a doctorate in philosophy and focused much of his graduate study on unintelligibility and nonsense. When he began to hear unusual stories from patients who had died and were then revived, he became intrigued.

The stories he heard from his patients followed patterns very similar to those of nonsense stories he had studied as a philosophy student. Much like the characters in *Alice in Wonderland*, his patients were saying things that seemed to challenge the usual notions of space and time; and like Lewis Carroll's characters, Moody's patients often spoke in puzzling paradoxes. Some of the things he heard from patients who had died and come back to life were sentences like these:

"There was time, but no time."

"I felt more alive when I was dead than when I was living."

"I understood everything everyone said, but not a word was spoken."

"I left my body and traveled through the galaxies, all while I was lying motionless in bed."

"It felt like it took a minute, but it also felt like a thousand years."

All of these sentences are paradoxical. How is it possible that something felt like a journey through the galaxies when, indeed, the patient lay motionless in bed, or felt like a minute but also a thousand years? These were intriguing statements, and as he heard paradoxical descriptions from his patients, he became increasingly curious about them. How could it be that a patient who came back to life reported never feeling as alive as when he was dead?

Over the course of years, as Moody wrote down accounts of these changes in the language and experiences of his patients, a pattern emerged that he identified as the near-death experience. Through his patients' "nonsensical stories," he pinpointed a unique set of experiences shared by some who had died and come back to life. Moody was particularly drawn to their narratives because their stories clearly described some kind of journey even though there had actually been no real movement from point A to point B, as we understand motion in three-dimensional reality. The stories that emerged were technically nonsense travel narratives. That is, in terms of the literal reality we know, the stories were nonsensical. The "journeys" these patients described having taken during their near-death experiences violate almost everything we know about our three-dimensional and five-sense world.

A closer look at these patterns of language associated with near-death experiences reveals a foundation for understanding the language of dying.

The Nonsense Travel Narrative

Those who have had near-death experiences often describe a kind of journey that occurs outside of their physical bodies, and their descriptions involve one or all of the following: (a) moving up and out of one's body, (b) moving through tunnels or valleys, and (c) meeting with deceased relatives or friends or spiritual figures and having a life review.

One of the features of a near-death experience (NDE) is that the person "moves up and out of the body" and has an "out-of-body experience"; this appears to be true whether a person reports a positive or a distressing NDE. The following description comes from John, one of the people I interviewed. He had a near-death experience after being taken to the hospital following a near-fatal car accident. His description is typical of the language people use as they speak about their out-of-body experiences: "The next thing I was aware of was floating on the ceiling of the hospital room. I could see everything that was going on below me — and even noticed the chalky white color of the ceiling." Within the context of our understanding of this three-dimensional, five-sense world, his description is nonsense, since in our literal world people do not float out of their bodies or have the ability to closely examine the ceiling paint while they are motionless on a bed below. However, those who describe their out-of-body experiences will tell you that although the language may seem nonsensical, the experience is intelligible and meaningful to them. "While those below were having conversations about my being dead, I felt completely alive and conscious," John explained.

Here is another representative description, from Lisa, who had a near-death experience after a heart attack: "I could feel I was leaving my body, and I could see down below. I don't know how long I was up there. But then suddenly, it was like a hand came down to hold me; and that hand became the most incredible light as I lifted up."

Those who describe out-of-body experiences explain they felt a strong sense of self at that moment, as if they were fully conscious, even though those in the physical world could not hear them or see or feel their movements above their lifeless bodies.

Movements up and out of the body are strongly associated with near-death experiences. We will see in later chapters that the very description of moving upward while physically motionless is also characteristic of the language of the dying.

Another common landmark in the travel narrative of those who have had near-death experiences is a tunnel or valley of some kind. This description comes from Sandi, who sent an email to the Final Words Project describing her NDE this way: "The tunnel I am in seems soft and long as if I am moving through a tunnel of clouds. I am ecstatic to be free and able to move with such grace and agility — to move so quickly. I am unburdened, unrestricted. Finally, I am myself again. As I go through the tunnel, I am moving toward the most beautiful golden light. I am home."

Even when told in past tense, these accounts convey motion, a powerful counterpoint to the reality of the individuals' lifeless bodies. This is clear in the testimony by Rick, who described his near-death experience that occurred after he was admitted to the hospital for sepsis. "I had the feeling I was moving through a very deep, dim valley. But I felt no fear. I actually felt comfort."

Guides for the Journey

Those who share their near-death experiences often speak of encounters with family members and friends who had died before them, and who greeted them or guided them in their journey. They also speak of spiritual figures, or "beings of light." Rick, for example, stated, "All these people were there. Many of them I had known and recognized, including a friend I knew back in elementary school. I felt their presence, and with some of them, I actually saw their bodies. I felt they all were welcoming me and wanted to protect or guide me."

Lisa explained further about her experience of a hand that lifted her up after her heart attack: "This Divine Presence was all light. And that light seemed to speak to me, to tell me he would be guiding me now. I trusted that presence completely."

On Christmas Day 1993, Shawna Ristic was in a serious car accident that pushed her near death and left her in a coma for many days. "I had a choice to come back or not," she said, "and this decision was a joint decision between myself and the council, a group of twelve beings I met during my time on the other side. I learned that I am working with and representing them here on earth. I saw the ramifications of both choices, the peace of staying with the beings full of light and love that had lovingly lifted me from my body."

References to "beings of light," deceased friends and relatives, and other guiding figures appear not only in the descriptions of those who have had near-death experiences but also, as we will see, in the accounts recorded by the Final Words Project.

The Journey Culminates in Life Review

Many who have had a near-death experience explain that the journey out of their body, guided by spiritual figures, friends, or family, led them to a life review. This review covers the complete span of the person's life and is often seen from the point of view of someone she or he had harmed.

Metaphoric language frequently appears in descriptions of these life reviews. In fact, those who recount their experiences say there is no way to explain the review process without resorting to analogies and symbols of this "afterlife" process. The metaphoric descriptions that I heard ranged from "It was like watching a movie" to "There were posts on rolling hills, and each post held an important landmark of my life; and it then came to life" to "It was as if there were globes, or spheres, like bubbles, that held images from my life."

The near-death experience itself is often described as a story or journey and shares the same landmarks: moving up, looking down and perceiving the deathbed scenes below, traveling through a tunnel, meeting with predeceased friends or family or spiritual figures, and then traveling to or through a life review and "arriving back" at the body.

When we look closely at the language of these exceptional experiences, we see a clear evolution away from literal language to language that is both rich in metaphor and paradoxical or nonsensical. The accounts associated with near-death experiences have many of the critical markers that also exist in the language of the dying. We hear a travel story, a journey filled with symbolic and paradoxical statements and which offers the possibility of traveling to or through another state of being or dimension where the rules of our literal three-dimensional, five-sense world no longer exist. The language we hear is often non-sense-ical — not grounded in the senses as we know them — and promotes a whole new understanding.

The Near-Death Experience Is Ineffable

The travel narrative is at the heart of the near-death experience, but those who have been through it will tell you that even the journey analogy does not quite reflect their experience. That is, there are no words to explain it. Every aspect that the person undergoes in those moments of clinical death defies description. Near-death experiencers universally explain that we simply cannot use the words or the points of reference to which we are accustomed. One of the first quotes documenting a near-death experience appeared in Raymond Moody's *Life After Life*. While spoken several decades ago, it succinctly summarizes a common sentiment of NDEers:

> Now, there is a real problem for me as I'm trying to tell you this because all the words I know are three-dimensional. As I was going through this, I kept thinking, "Well, when I was taking geometry, they always told me there were only three dimensions, and I always just accepted that. But they were wrong. There are more." And, of course, our world — the one we're living in now — *is* three-dimensional, but the next one definitely isn't. And that's why it's so hard to tell you this. I have to describe it to you in words that are three-dimensional. That's as close as I can get to it, but it's not really adequate. I can't really give you a complete picture.

In my interviews with near-death experiencers, I heard the same theme: the experience defies the words or reality we all share here. Language cannot convey something that goes beyond the five senses.

Metaphors Allow Us to Describe the Ineffable

The ineffable quality of the language of the other side makes it necessary for near-death experiencers to reach for figurative speech or even nonsense, such as "like floating through clouds," "like the frames of a movie," "like entering a big dark house with the lights on for the first time," "like living inside the colors of a high-definition television," and "like arriving home." Descriptions by near-death experiencers all demonstrate that metaphor is the only way these individuals can explain something that is so different from our ordinary experience; NDEers can only begin to convey, through metaphor and analogies, what they perceived. This is an important thing to remember as we look at the highly metaphoric language that emerges in the language of the dying.

As discussed earlier in this chapter, we have access to a continuum of language. Literal language is the language of our shared reality in this five-sense world. Metaphors, then, help us articulate experiences that seem to originate beyond our five senses and this three-dimensional reality. Perhaps, then, it is no surprise that metaphors appear frequently in the language of near-death experiences — and at the end of life.

Figures of speech, such as metaphors, reflect the power of language to both alter our reality and create bridges to new ones. Figures of speech can take us out of the ordinary and expand our awareness through the use of comparisons. Moody notes that figures of speech are common in the descriptions of NDEs, as it is impossible to relate NDEs without engaging certain "special effects of language."

The Language of Near Death
Is Often Paradoxical

Language is sequential, but the near-death experience is often described as having no spatial or temporal sequence. This non-sequential quality of the near-death experience makes it necessary for people to reach not only for metaphorical but also for paradoxical descriptions like those mentioned earlier.

Most of the people I interviewed explained that the past, present, and future coexisted all at once. Many explained that the more they tried to capture their experience with language, the more confused they felt and the less coherent their explanations became. Our bodies and language function, it seems, to organize experience and thought in a way that follows a linear narrative. But beyond our living bodies, a more vast nonlinear, nonnarrative reality exists. Here is a summary of the kinds of paradoxical phrases I have heard during my research into the language of near-death experiences — the very kinds of statements that first piqued the interest of Raymond Moody over forty years ago:

> "When I was dead, I felt better than I had ever felt in my life."
>
> "We communicated with complete understanding, but no one spoke a word."
>
> "The Divine Presence showed me that the real world is not *really* real."

Of the many paradoxical statements associated with the near-death experience, those associated with the research of Kenneth Ring and Sharon Cooper are among the most dramatic. They studied the near-death experiences of thirty-one blind participants. Of those, 80 percent described being able to "see" while clinically dead. They described details of the weather and of the clothing and accessories of hospital staff, patients, and themselves. The blind can *see?* This paradoxical statement makes no sense in our usual, five-sense world. The paradoxical language associated with near-death experiences suggests that there is a dimension or reality that cannot be fully explained in the language with which most of us are comfortable.

Moody notes that the phrase *life after death* itself violates common logic, because it is paradoxical. He suggests a logic of unintelligibility that allows for death and life to exist concurrently.

Aristotelian logic is binary, he explains. However, there is the un-intelligible dimension that seems not to fall into the true-or-false world of Aristotle. The language of those who experience NDEs appears to reflect this unintelligible dimension. The language of the threshold may be governed by its own logic that is only barely comprehensible to most of us.

At present, there is no physiological or psychological model that alone can explain all the common features of NDEs. The occurrence of awareness and clarity during a period of impaired cerebral functioning remains a paradox. How is it that some people can experience clear consciousness outside the body during a period of clinical death, when the brain, no longer functioning, registers a flatline EEG? It's as if the brain in this state were a computer with its power source unplugged and its circuits removed. How could such a computer process information at all? Nonetheless, during an NDE some patients have experienced lucidity while their brains and bodies were clinically dead.

The Language of the Afterlife Is Telepathic

Eben Alexander, the neurosurgeon who authored *Proof of Heaven*, tells us that communication on the other side is not only paradoxical but also "nonlinguistic." According to those who have died and returned, there appears to be no sequential time, fixed space, or spoken language as we know it.

All of those I interviewed described communication that took place during the NDE as telepathic. Commonly, they explained what happened as being something like this: "I hear them talk about me as I rise out of my body. I hear the words 'We lost him. He is dead.' And then I am still able to understand them, but in a new way." Near-death experiencers often explain that they understood perfectly what was being communicated at their deathbed. However, there is an important shift in how people explain "hearing."

For example, one person told me: "The voices were not really audible in the way we think of it. It's more like I became aware of what people were thinking, and suddenly communication was between our minds — telepathic."

Many NDEers may have even experienced precognition as they left their bodies. Several of them made comments like "I was aware of what the doctor was saying before he spoke." Usually, this is the point when people realize they are no longer living. Then a new kind of consciousness awakens, and this process inevitably leads to the cessation of spoken words. Bret had this to say about the communication in his near-death experience: "My mother spoke to me, and I understood everything. I was supposed to follow her. But there were no real words giving me instructions — not the way we think of words. I just knew that I was to follow her — her whole being communicated."

Several of the people who described their NDEs to me, including Shawna, who was mentioned earlier in this chapter, explained that they were introduced to a divine being or council who discussed whether the person should return to the life left behind. These conversations are always described as being "unspoken" — that is, concepts and emotions were expressed "nonlinguistically," in Eben Alexander's term.

Many of the telepathic conversations that NDEers reported took place with predeceased friends, family members, or a Divine Presence or light and were about whether to "go back." In most cases, people explain that they experienced "mind-to-mind" or "heart-to-heart communication" that went far beyond what we know as spoken language. It would be easy to ascribe all this to mere imagination; however, there are multiple cases in which NDEers comprehended communications by doctors, nurses, and loved ones, even though, by all clinical measures, they could no longer hear. As explained earlier, people have described hearing the living not through audible language but through thought — that is, telepathically.

In some instances people communicated with relatives or friends they did not know were dead but encountered during their after-life experience. Interestingly, many of those who have had near-death experiences explain that, after having died and come back to life, they retain some ability to communicate telepathically and enjoy increased intuitive ability. Sandi described it this way: "But now I am home, communicating telepathically without effort." Palliative-care nurse and researcher Madelaine Lawrence and several other researchers, including Kenneth Ring and Sharon Cooper, have documented these findings, as have members of the International Association for Near-Death Studies and the Near Death Experience Research Foundation.

Lawrence tells us, "As the person in the transpersonal experience moves away from earthly situations, auditory communication is more likely to be telepathic. Vision is enhanced during the ethereal part of the NDE, including the ability of blind individuals to see.... These results are consistent for thousands of subjects at this time across cultures."

Could it be that the continuum of language ends in telepathic communication?

Let's take a look at how the continuum of language evident in near-death experiences emerges in the language of the dying.

CHAPTER THREE

Metaphors of the Momentous

Before We Die, We Announce a Big Event

What are we celebrating? Oh! Celebration party!
Dear, dear, dear. Is this a holiday?
— *Judy, Final Words Project participant*

In chapter 2, we talked about the power of metaphor to help us describe things that do not fit our ordinary experience and cannot be fully explained through literal language. We saw how metaphor frequently emerges in the language of near-death experience because it offers speakers a way to communicate about ineffable experiences through comparisons and analogies.

End-of-life language, too, is highly metaphoric. The following examples of metaphors are veiled expressions alerting listeners that a major event is approaching. My father spoke about the big art exhibition, and many Final Words Project participants shared end-of-life metaphors that announced the coming of a big event. The symbols of the major event are usually connected to the life narrative or interests of the speaker.

Andrea posted this on the Final Words Project's Facebook page: "On the night my aunt died from lung cancer, she was clearly between two worlds. Her last words to me were when she asked me to bring her best dress and shoes to the hospital because she was attending a grand ball that night and would be so happy to see me there. She died the next day."

A young man, Thomas, shared this on Facebook: "My grandmother woke up in the middle of the night and started getting dressed in a long gown that was in the back of the closet. She was sitting at her dressing table, putting on jewelry and makeup. An aide came in to see what was going on. My grandma said, 'Why, I am getting ready for the big dance!' She then lay down on the bed and died."

One beloved told his wife, "Dave is telling me he's waiting for me. He's waiting to play golf with me. They need a fourth."

Another dying husband shared the following with his partner: "Through you, we're in touch with the headquarters of the operation of the aircraft....I may well be coming to a special moment, and that is…we have to let it go at…that point…"

Hospice worker and health-care providers I interviewed all agreed that the language of their dying patients is often highly metaphoric, a quality made clear by the examples above. "They are an individual's unique, personal 'heads-up' to herald impending transition," explained nurse Becki Hawkins. "An avid golfer may say something to this effect: 'I have a golf game scheduled for tomorrow.' It doesn't seem to make sense at the time, but later it does!"

Carol emailed the Final Words Project with an account of the last words of her father, a roofing contractor: "He would awaken and look over at me and smile so big. And he told me, 'They have all these kitchenettes over there!' There were miles and miles of them, and he would be helping build them." For some, the world they enter beyond the threshold is filled with new construction; others find the steady beat of dance.

Leo Holder, son of renowned dancer and choreographer Geoffrey Holder, wrote this description of his father's final words:

Then his right hand starts to move…then the left hand begins tapping. Through the oxygen mask, the gurgling starts creating its own rhythm. Not sure of what I'm hearing, I look up to see his mouth moving. I get closer to listen: "…two, three…two, three…" He's counting! It gets stronger, and at its loudest sounds like the deep purr of a lion, then he says, "Arms, two, three…Turn, two, three… Swing, two, three…Down, two, three…"

In another story, Doug C. Smith, a hospice director in West Virginia, talked about his patient Jack, a retired vaudeville magician:

As I stood in the doorway of his hospital room, I saw Jack propped upright, surrounded by pillows. He smiled and said, "Doug. We have all been waiting for you to arrive."

I wondered who "we" were, because he was the only person in the room. I walked in, smiled at him, and thought this might not be such a difficult visit after all.

"Today is your initiation day, Doug. Today you will become a member of the Royal Society of Magicians," Jack said.

This was going to be a fun visit, I thought, and I wanted to participate in his fun.

But Jack then looked away from me, and his expression seemed glassy-eyed. He spoke several nonsensical sentences sounding both like a magical incantation and a "speaking in tongues."

He abruptly broke off his nonsensical language and looked directly at me. "Come closer," he said in a serious tone. "You will learn a great magic trick today. The very greatest trick of all."

His voice was weak but determined: "Come closer."

I felt that I was already near enough to hear whatever he was about to do or say, but I leaned in, over his bed.

"Come closer," he repeated.

I began to feel uncomfortable, but I leaned in until we were eye to eye with no more than six inches between our faces.

Jack seemed to be looking straight through me. His eyes were searching for something in my eyes. Without any change in his facial expression, Jack whispered, "Watch me disappear."

His eyes took on a glassy, frozen appearance. I knew instantly that Jack died in the moment he whispered those words.

This powerful account illustrates how the dying engage the metaphors of their lives as they cross into the Great Mystery. Metaphors help us equate what is unknown with what is known — and can offer us comfort and a reference point as we make sense of extraordinary experiences. This may be why our natural environment, like our lifetime career, offers a familiar touch point that emerges in final words, foreshadowing a big event. Metaphors about a change in environmental conditions feature in the accounts of several people who shared last words with me:

> "The big storm is coming."
>
> "I think the rain is coming. Do you think it is going to rain?"
>
> "The tide is turning."

Signature Metaphors for Seeking Completion

Not only do we hear the dying speak of an important event coming, but we also hear metaphors that suggest seeking completion or wholeness.

An avid golfer announces that a big tournament is coming —
and then elaborates upon this metaphor, explaining that he is playing with a threesome, all of whom are deceased, and that he will be
making it a foursome. The theme of foursomes appears repeatedly
in the transcripts of my interviews: we are told by the person dying
that he or she is called to be the fourth, whether for a poker game
or a golf tournament. So while these particular activities reflect the
individual's interests, the theme of threes and fours may have more
archetypal significance.

Shannon shared these words that her grandfather spoke when
approaching death: "These three men are playing poker and they
keep asking me to be the fourth hand. They want me to come and
drink and smoke with them. I'm telling them I'm not interested. I
want to stay right where I am in my chair. I am telling them I don't
want to play. I don't want to join in their game."

According to Carl Jung, the number three in dreams represents
transformation, while four indicates wholeness, so joining a threesome, and becoming the fourth player, may relate to seeking completion as the dying person completes her or his life.

In the language of the dying, there is also a variety of references to two becoming one, such as this one from a lover of boats:
"There are two hulls, and I need you to get the two hulls, need to
put them together to make one." Another with the theme of wholeness: "What you see in different pieces...it's all in one piece." And
another: "There's a circle on the left...and a circle on the right...
these two circles make one."

"It's not clear if the dying person knows what is real or not
real," nurse and researcher Madelaine Lawrence remarked to me
during an interview. "The line between the metaphor and the reality is blurred."

Whether the dying know what is real or not, what is most important is that they are engaged in a process of making sense of

the reality before them. As they do so, themes of completion and wholeness appear to be significant — and for each of us, the symbols and metaphors may be different.

Kelly Bulkeley and Rev. Patricia Bulkley, the authors of *Dreaming beyond Death*, tell us that as they studied people's dream journals they found that over time the same symbols and themes repeated themselves: "Each of us has our own set of signature dream themes that recur throughout our lives. What this and other studies suggest is that dreams not only mirror the ups and downs of daily life, they also reflect the enduring qualities of our personality and the foundational concerns that shape our way of being in the world."

This principle of dreams is also true of the dreamlike state many enter at the end of life. The metaphors we use as we approach death are often closely connected to the themes central to us throughout our lives. Even as our thought processes and language appear to change, the themes and central symbols often do not.

Similarly, cultural metaphors, too, may appear in language at the end of life, since we cannot separate who we are as individuals from the culture we live in. Linguist George Lakoff tells us that in American English there are two primary metaphors for the mind. The first one is the idea that "the mind is a brittle object," as in these examples: "He broke under cross-examination," "His mind snapped," and "I am going to pieces." The second central metaphor for the mind is the idea that "the mind is a machine," as in these phrases: "My mind is not operating today" or "Boy, the wheels are turning!"

It is not surprising, then, to see these cultural metaphors emerge in transcripts of the Final Words Project that describe things breaking down or coming apart, as in these examples:

"My modality is broken."
"I need maintenance for this."

"I need time to get everything in order."

"Everything in pieces...so many pieces."

"I got to put this all back together."

"Dear, our connection in the north has made an error,
      has made a wrong turn."

The phrase "I need to put things in order" emerges in several of the transcripts from my research — and boxes are a recurring symbol of putting things in order. Here's one example:

Then she started talking about the five boxes that she needed to organize and get all together. She started talking about where she could put them all and was worried [about whether] these five boxes would be all right. I was trying to make sense of what she might be talking about, but then it became clear to me that she has five children. So I thought maybe the boxes were somehow a metaphor for her children.

With agitation, she said, "I need to find a place for them!"

I started naming all the places where each of us lived: "How about Ohio, Mom? New Mexico?" She continued to be agitated. I then said, "I know the perfect place! How about we keep them in your heart?"

She liked that and seemed relieved, "Yes, I will keep them there!"

Boxes appeared in several of the transcripts, including my father's. Why a box? Interestingly enough, it's a container often used for moving and as a way to organize things, and it has four corners. Is there an association here, too, with the theme of four and completion?

Metaphors Evolve during the Dying Process

Martha Jo Atkins, a death educator and author of the book *Signposts of Dying*, told me that in her experience, the metaphors that people utter evolve as death nears. She explained that someone might first indicate that something is needed or is missing, for example, "I need my map..." That may change to "Who has my suitcase? I need my suitcase." Later the individual may say, "My suitcase is packed. I am ready to go now."

Atkins has heard a whole range of metaphors, many of them related to travel, and many connected to meals or to the table being set. "Then the wine is poured," Atkins related, "and sooner or later, the big dinner is announced." The following example is typical of several I heard during my Final Words Project research: "I need a shower today. Get me cleaned up. Where's the aide? I need to get ready. I've got to get ready for the dinner! Can't you see? The table is set."

One woman explained to me that she had offered her husband some grapefruit juice at the end of breakfast, asking if he would like some more. "No, I am done," he said and, seconds later, died — an example of the metaphor of the meal.

This same kind of evolution of metaphors and symbols occurs in dreams before death. Kelly Bulkeley and Rev. Patricia Bulkley explain that dreams help us work through our fears and anxieties as death approaches, just as they have assisted us in navigating other major transitions in our life. Dreams offer up images that allow the transformation of fear and anxiety and lead to spiritual insight or emotional breakthrough. Like the evolving metaphors in our language, our dream symbols develop through the course of our final days to help us attain peace, reconcile with the reality before us, and reach closure in our relationships with others.

Carolyn shared her husband's final words with me, which were attuned to a major shift in the weather and a major change in his condition:

> During the last two days, as he entered the transition time, he kept repeating the words "The reservoirs are filling." That was before this big storm, and now I wonder if he was actually aware of its coming, seeing from a wider perspective already. The last time he said those words, he added, "That's good. But…it also doesn't really matter." I responded with something like: "Because you now are seeing two worlds." And his response was: "Oh, many more than two!"

We move between realities or dimensions, between dream time and literal reality, as we make sense of what is occurring to us. At a time when symbolic and metaphorical language has such potency, it would make sense to engage metaphor in ways to enhance end-of-life care. Researchers with the Metaphor in End-of-Life Care project in England are doing exactly that. These researchers found that many medical practitioners were using the metaphor of "battling illness and defeating it," a metaphor that inevitably leads to perceiving dying as a defeat. For many, this was a painful way to map the inevitability of death. When the primary metaphor is, in contrast, a journey, then every step along the way offers an opportunity for personal growth, resolution, and exploration. This study has shaped public health policy in the United Kingdom, where doctors and nurses are advised to communicate with families of the dying by using the analogy of a journey rather than that of a battle. From what they learned about metaphor, they discovered that language matters.

Stephen Jones, a community education coordinator for Hospice of Santa Barbara, shared this story about the importance of being attuned to the metaphors and symbols of those we care for:

> One morning a staff caregiver was freshening up a resident's room. When she got over to the dresser, she noticed a vase of wilted daisies. When the caregiver reached for them, the woman in bed spoke up shyly: "I know that my flowers are dying, but you are not going to throw them out, are you?" she asked softly. Recognizing what the dried-out flowers meant to Joanne, the caregiver said kindly, "Well, then, let's get them into some fresh water, shall we?" She then brought the bouquet bedside so Joanne could watch the petals drop. "They die so beautifully, don't they?" she said, picking up a petal between her own wilted fingers.

Metaphors and Dreams

Dream expert Robert J. Hoss relates end-of-life metaphors to physiology and the function of dreams. He explained that the "logical mind" and speech centers are inactive when we dream. The images we see in dreams do not have the same identity or rational meaning as in waking life. It could be that this is true also as we are dying. During dreaming, the parts of the brain that are highly active draw upon our memories to resolve or make sense of problems or issues in our lives. This could explain why we engage the metaphors of our lives as we struggle to make sense of the overwhelming reality facing us. Hoss remarked, "What better picture of the pending trauma than a 'storm coming' or a 'door closing' or 'windows bringing in the light' or even 'broken machinery'? What better way to represent getting ready for the next life than 'getting ready for the big dance or event'?"

The part of the brain that creates the dream can speak only in pictures. So all of our thoughts at the time of death are converted into pictures that represent those thoughts; many are personal pictures from our memories, and some are cultural. When people are going through the greatest transformation in their lives — that of dying — these images frequently show up in their dreams and, perhaps by extension, in their language.

Shamanic and mystical traditions present a slightly different perspective. They describe the world of dreams as the world that intersects with the "other side" or another dimension. Shannon Willis, a counselor, dream expert, and student of shamanism, explained in an interview with me that there are many kinds of dreams. Among them are those that help us make sense of life events and offer images to help us transform how we feel about ourselves and the future.

Willis added, however, that in many shamanic and spiritual traditions, dreams are viewed as an interface to the realm of the ancestors. Among the aboriginal peoples of Australia and the South Pacific, tribal communities of Africa, and native peoples of North and South America, dreams have been regarded as a primary means of maintaining contact with the spirits of the dead. This was also true among ancient civilizations in China, India, Egypt, and Greece. In dreams, people travel to otherworldly realms and gain important knowledge and wisdom.

If, indeed, the dream state intersects with another dimension or "the other side," this might help us better understand the premonitions and visitations revealed in final conversations, which I discuss further in later chapters.

Explained shaman Mandy Peat, "When a shaman journeys to the spirit world, whether that be the upper, middle, or below world, we see, hear, and feel with symbols. So as we approach death, our minds and consciousness are being expanded to prepare us for multidimensional dialogue and experiences. Quite literally, we lose our minds and enter a higher level of consciousness expressed through the symbolic and metaphoric language — the language of higher realities."

As we die, we enter into a dreamlike state, and we live partly there and partly in the world of waking reality. The language of dream time — like the language of dying — is a language all its own. Whether this realm is a portal to another dimension or simply another mental state in which we transform our fears and rehearse our unknowable futures, I am not certain. I do know, however, that we have access to these two realms throughout our lives, and that this access seems to intensify throughout the dying process, as our metaphoric and symbolic language indicates.

As I thought about this, I looked at a recent entry from my journal, composed after I'd had a disturbing dream about crows. I read over the words I had written in the middle of the night while apparently still grounded in the world of dreams. The words I used were so different from the language of waking and literal reality:

> I dreamt ten black crows came to me. They woke me with their claws digging into my chest. I sat up in bed and whispered to John, "I saw ten black crows land on me. Do you think that means I am going to die soon?"
>
> He smiled, "It's a murder…a murder…of crows…" and rolled back to sleep.
>
> I invited the black crows to speak with me, and they followed me to the woods beyond the creek out back and each crow took a turn telling me its story. And the last black crow had the eyes of my father and sat above me like a guardian. He told me it was okay now. I would let the light shine in the lantern. He would stand watch. I listened closely and took note.

Some cultures teach that we should listen to and honor images like these that emerge in dreams. Listening to the dying can be like this listening. I wrote the following in my journal as I reflected on the dream-time quality of one of the accounts I'd heard earlier in the day:

In the hour before dawn as the light of the moon ended and morning's twilight had just begun its new journey, in that hour between dark and dawn, the world was silent except in the room where Karen Lewis sat amid the soft clicks and hums of machines and the rhythmic drip of the IV, next to the man she loved. She awaited a sign or word, or reemergence from his deep coma. And then suddenly there was a stirring, right before the sun rose. Karen could barely believe what she saw as the covers moved themselves and her lover rose like a puppet pulled by strings from beyond. He turned to her and said, "Karen, it's not what you think." He quietly and gently lay back down, his sunken cheekbones prominent in the shadows.

The language of dream time — like the language of dying — is a language all its own. And it's not always what we think — just as the language of dreaming, as in my dream of the ten black crows, is filled with multiple meanings. The words of dreams are not simply understood in the same way as literal words, such as "The chair is made of oak."

CHAPTER FOUR

I Leave You with These Words

Travel Metaphors Speak of a Coming Voyage

> I've got to get off, get off!
> Off of this life.
> I'm dying. I'm dying.
> The trains keep going by.
> The trains keep going by, but I can't get on.
> I've got the ticket. I have the ticket.
> — *James, Final Words Project participant*

Remarkable metaphors emerge in the voices of the dying. Engaging the metaphors that are meaningful to our beloveds can lead to healing conversations. Speaking of death as a journey instead of a battle, for example, offers a way to frame the dying process that is more about exploration and discovery than it is about defeat.

The metaphor of the journey is a centerpiece in the language of the dying. People speak about reaching the end of one journey and, in some cases, about heading out to another. Words about transportation and vehicles abound. Annette, my dental hygienist, shared her grandmother's final words with me:

"Yellow bus! There's the bus."
"Who is driving that bus, Grandma?"
"Not sure. Not sure…but lots of angels!"

Much like the metaphors of the momentous in the previous chapter, the symbols of travel relate specifically to the person's life. Annette's grandmother was a long-term churchgoer, and angels figured heavily in the images that surrounded her in life. People who love sailing or cruises may speak about boats or ships awaiting them. My father, who had a passion for gambling, announced a few weeks before his death: "We have a long flight ahead to Las Vegas."

A hospice nurse was confused when she first heard a patient ask, "Where's my Jetta? Where's my Jetta?" Then she discovered that he owned a Volkswagen Jetta. She reassured him that it was "all gassed up and ready for you." A few days later, he died.

"Are my bags packed? The train is coming soon. I got to be ready. I'm looking for the platform. Where is the platform?" one woman's brother asked her.

Of all the analogies I have heard associated with dying, not one has been about heading out for a long stroll or jog. While a couple of people have said, "Get my coat; I have to go," no one yet has been recorded as saying, "Get my tennies. I am preparing for a long walk." The transportation metaphors involve outside agency — someone or something beyond our own physical body transports us. One exception was this phrase, repeated several times by one woman close to death: "It's a hop, skip, and a jump away." However, this may have been less about how she was "traveling" and more about the use of an idiom to express the immediacy of her dying.

Typical are phrases such as "Take me to the bus station. It's time to go home now" and "The boat has arrived for me." Or, as mentioned earlier, some express their need for a passport. Hospice nurses tell me that metaphors like these are prevalent in patients no matter what their specific diagnosis, medication, or physical condition as death approaches.

The Prevalence of the Journey Metaphor

The metaphor of death as a journey is deeply rooted in who and what we are. This is true not only of us as individuals but also of human beings collectively, since the metaphor emerges in languages and cultures throughout the world. Here are some examples: in Afrikaans, people speak of going to the goat field; in Dutch, of going out of the pipe; in German, of going to the eternal hunting grounds; in Hebrew, of descending to the afterworld; in Hungarian, of leaving for the eternal hunting fields; in Irish, of going on the path of truth; in Spanish, of going on a tour, passing on to a better life, or moving to a face-up neighborhood; in Portuguese, of going upstairs; and in Romanian, of turning at the corner. The Danish, too, use the phrase "to turn a corner." Interestingly, one English speaker I interviewed shared the fact that her father's final words were "How far to the corner? Where I take a right, where I used to live." In Chinese, when people hint at someone's dying, they talk about "knocking on death's door." While it may not represent the language of travel, it suggests that a door is opening into a new place.

Consider these words from a man at the threshold who announces that he is on a pilgrimage. The metaphor of the track evokes the sensation of going somewhere; he is pulling away, it seems, from the station: "For those who do not choose, the rest of us on this pilgrimage bid you a temporary or permanent farewell....Anyone that wishes, take a hand and pull gently backward so the pilgrimage will be on the right track. Gently pull, gently pull, and we will begin to move away."

Kelly Bulkeley and Rev. Patricia Bulkley found that dreams of journeys are common, and that these often transform people's fear of dying into a sense of adventure or awe. This example from their book illustrates the power of a traveling dream: "I am sailing again at night in uncharted waters and the old sense of adventure comes back. I feel the tingle of excitement again, of pushing through the waves in the vast, dark, empty sea but knowing somehow I am right on course. And strangely enough, I'm not afraid to die anymore. In fact, I feel ready to go, more so every day."

Their clinical observations were confirmed by a 2014 study of the visions and dreams of the dying, in which hospice patients were asked to describe what they had dreamed about. In this longitudinal study, the authors found that almost 40 percent of the participants dreamed of going, or preparing to go, somewhere.

Could it be that the increase in metaphoric language reflects a voyage away from this literal five-sense, three-dimensional reality in preparation for another — an experience that is impossible to put into literal language?

Jeanne Van Bronkhorst tells us that two important messages appear in the dreams of the dying, and these are closely related to what we hear in final conversations: "The first is the calm, direct, occasionally visceral assertion that the body will die. In these dreams, things break down, doctors walk away shaking their heads, the dreamer hears there is nothing more to be done." The other message concerns how the dreamer is "traveling to a new place, meeting old and cherished friends again, and finding help and comfort from someplace beyond physical life."

The metaphors we hear may represent a real journey that awaits us, or a whole new territory of experience, as we each approach the new experience of death. It could be that we substitute the analogies of the odyssey, something that is known, as we try to make sense of the frightening and unknown experience of dying.

As people die, many enter a world in which language functions in a new way. It is no longer primarily a tool for communicating about our shared literal reality. Instead, it acts as a vehicle to transport us to a new one. Literal language gives way to a sense of motion that comes with these allusions to travel. These shifts are reminiscent of what we heard in the nonsense travel narratives of near-death experiences.

The Journey of Life

The metaphor of life as a journey figures prominently in the accounts of those who have had near-death experiences. They tell us that throughout life, we examine life as a forward-moving narrative, an odyssey that moves us toward an end; however, when we are near death, that narrative suddenly changes, and we look back in time to make sense of the journey through life. During the life review, mentioned in chapter 2, near-death experiencers are (a) shown or told the importance of gleaning lessons from their life odyssey, and (b) asked to review life's events through the eyes of others in order to deepen their ability to love and have compassion. The tales of NDEers tell us that life is a journey, and that our primary mission is to learn to love.

The happiest lives are framed by narratives that allow us to imagine we have made progress, that we have moved from one place to another, that our lives have a beginning, middle, and end. The journey metaphor emerges from the symbolic importance of the odyssey, and it offers us the chance to frame the end in a larger, more consoling narrative. Donald Miller, in his book *A Million Miles in a Thousand Years*, writes about the structure of stories and our lives: "It's like this with every crossing, and with nearly every story too. You paddle until you no longer believe you can go any further. And then suddenly, well after you thought it would happen, the shore starts to grow, and it grows fast. The trees get taller and you can make out the crags in the cliffs, and then the shore reaches out to you, to welcome you home, almost pulling your boat onto the sand." It seems from the language of the dying that the voyage undertaken offers us hope that we will arrive on some other side. Among the consoling aspects of a story is the fact that the main character is transformed after challenges — and usually for the better. The potential for positive transformation makes our journeys — and our life stories — worth it.

In their 2015 research into the last words of 407 death row inmates in Texas, investigators discovered that the final utterances contained a significantly higher proportion of positive than negative emotion words. In our informal research through the Final Words Project, we found the same thing. In the death row research, the inmates were, of course, not terminally ill, so many of the other natural processes associated with the end of life did not apply. However, the death row findings, coupled with those of the Final Words Project, suggest that something about the intensified awareness of our mortality turns our focus on what was good and right about our lives. This positive focus leads us to frame life as a journey. And the journey often is a teacher.

It could be that the increased frequency of positive words in the statements of the dying is an expression of a transpersonal awareness or understanding as we approach the threshold, whether we arrive there through terminal illness or lethal injection. That is, we see the whole perspective at the summit of the mountain with greater love and understanding. We are at the top, looking down, and suddenly the odyssey makes sense. We are standing at the same threshold that is reached by those who have near-death experiences. Suddenly life is simply a journey filled with lessons.

It may be similar to what happens after a monthlong road trip. We proudly share our photos with our friends and family, laugh as we share the stories of our challenges and conquests, and suddenly it all looks okay. The flat tire on the four-lane highway, or the bedbugs in the cheap hotel, or our fight with our drunk aunt Rita becomes a colorful landmark on an awe-inspiring adventure. The metaphor allows us to turn life's travails into travels. Our challenges are merely roadblocks, and our relationships and activities are landmarks on the journey, all with new lessons for us to learn about life on the road. The journey metaphor travels with us throughout life and apparently even after life, according to the accounts of near-death experiences.

We Not Only Depart, We Arrive

In accounts collected for the Final Words Project, we hear not only about departing but also about arriving. Common are exclamations about arriving and then finding individuals the dying person loved who preceded that person in death. One woman described her mother as saying, "It's time to get up, get up, get up…I am coming, Richard!" A nurse explained, "One of my patients last week said, 'Dad, I'm here!' His face smooth and almost smiling, he then said three times, 'He's leaving, he's leaving, he's leaving.' Then he passed away."

Others report hearing phrases like "I'm coming, Mother! I am ready now!" and "I need to get my coat. I am coming, Sarah." Still others describe moving toward something beautiful and looking forward to arriving there. For example, one said, "I have seen a beautiful light, and I was going toward it. I want to go into that light. It was so peaceful. I really had to fight to come back. I am not worried about tomorrow. And you shouldn't be. Promise me you won't worry."

Hospice nurse Barbara Green reported that one of her patients, a World War II veteran, had had a near-death experience during the war. He told her that, as a result, he had no fear of death. "He said that when he had died, he had felt complete peace and joy and was in a very beautiful place. He embraced death fully." He assured Barbara, "I am waiting to go home. I look forward to it." Later as he neared death, he asked her, "Why am I still here? I am waiting for my bus ticket. I am ready to go home."

We could explain away the language of departure as a metaphor for leaving this world, especially since the metaphor of a journey figures prominently throughout our lives for most of us. However, announcing our arrival at a place that has never before existed in the awareness of the speaker, and greeting those who have died before us, suggest that more than the comfort of a metaphor is at play here.

Do we speak of dying as a journey because we have no other means to make sense of the end of life? Or do we use the journey metaphor because there are no literal words to describe the passage we are making? Perhaps we are, indeed, boarding a train for a new destination, a place that can be described only in intensified and figurative language — a place so magnificent that it led Steve Jobs to exclaim, "Oh, wow! Oh, wow! Oh, wow!"

CHAPTER FIVE

Repetition, Repetition, Repetition
Intensified Language in Our Last Days

A place that is so beautiful, is shining like diamonds,
Mom, oh my God, Mom, so beautiful!
— *Daria, Final Words Project participant*

Repetition and exclamations are common at the end of life. Both are forms of intensified language that express extreme emotion or reaction. The last words of Steve Jobs, founder of the Apple corporation, are clearly an expression of intensified language. We can only imagine what inspired his final expression of awe. Perhaps his perception broadened to encompass the same magnificent landscape that moved Thomas Edison to emerge from a coma, open his eyes, look upward, and exclaim, "It is very beautiful over there!"

Exclamations of wonder occur frequently in the words of the dying, often in reference to someplace not visible to the living. Here are a few examples:

> "Do you hear that music? It is so beautiful! It is the most beautiful thing I have ever heard!"
> "The left. The left side. It is just like you described to me. But more beautiful!"

> "Oh, more…more…more worlds and worlds…and
>   worlds."
> "The green dimension! The green dimension!"
> "I'm happy. I'm happy!"
> "Beautiful, so beautiful!"

There are also expressions of intensified anguish or pain or fear, such as these last words from a young man's father:

> "I don't want to die! I don't want to die!"
> "I am scared to die. Help me! Help me!"

Repetition plays an important part in exclamations of both wonder and anguish. It is a form of figurative language that can turn a simple sentence into a dramatic one, making certain experiences more memorable. Repetition expresses intensified emotions, insight, knowing. It also deepens, deepens, deepens our point of focus.

Like a heartbeat.

A drumbeat.

Or the rhythm of cicadas or river currents or gulls calling.

The following beautiful description comes from my friend the author Carolyn North, who wrote about death and dying in *The Experience of a Lifetime: Living Fully, Dying Consciously*. In an email sent out to friends and family, Carolyn shared this account of her husband's final words:

> "It's good, but," he whispered at one point, "also not im-
> portant." It was very close to the end and I leaned forward
> to catch his words.
>
> "Because you see that there are two worlds?" I asked
> him quietly.
>
> "Oh, more…more…" Here he lifted an arm and de-
> scribed spirals in the air. "More worlds and worlds…" His

eyes were awestruck, seeing what the rest of us could not see. "Oh…so…profound," he whispered. "So…powerful."

Repetition has its own special effects, often increasing the power of emotion; it is capable of shifting our mental state. Repetition frames the importance — the *real* importance — of what is said, as is illustrated in these examples from literature and the Bible:

"O horror, horror, horror." — *Macbeth*
"Comfort ye, comfort ye my people." — Isaiah 40:1
"Words, words, words." — *Hamlet*

As we cross the threshold, repetition appears in a number of ways. We saw earlier that it is used often in declarations of wonder; but it is also used to express a number of other themes. Here are some typical kinds of pronouncements that I encountered:

Reassurance

"I feel secure. I feel so secure."
"Tell everyone I am all right. I am all right."
"There is no fear…no fear…no fear."

Gratitude

"I have to thank them. I want to thank them. I want to thank them."
"Thank you, thank you, thank you. I love you."

The End

"I am dying, I am dying, and there are all these people here."
"I am dying. I am dying."
"I am daring…daring, daring to die."
"Bye. Bye. Bye now."

Resistance

"Go away! Go away! I am not ready yet!"

"I don't want to die! I don't want to die!"

"I am tired. So tired. I am losing it. Losing it."

"It's so hard to die! It's so hard to die!"

Unity

"There are two hulls, and I need you to get the two hulls, need to put them together to make one."

"It's all in one piece…It's all in one piece…It's all in one piece…What you see in different pieces…it's all in one piece!"

Circles

"It's a circle…it's a circle…love is a circle."

"The circles say it's time to complete the cycle."

"Like those circles at the top of the Christmas tree. A small circle inside a larger one."

Numerics

"What is the number 8 doing in the corner of my room? What is the number 8…down there?"

"Three days left. Three days left. I know I have three left. But my family won't let me. They won't."

"Enough…enough…the angels say enough…only three days left."

Circles appear frequently in final words, often in enigmatic and mysterious ways. They imply completeness or wholeness, as does unity (examples of which precede the circle examples in the list). I have not heard anyone say, "It's a square! It's a square!" or "It's a hexagon! It's a hexagon." (Notice the common use of *it's* in the language of the threshold, which I explore in more detail in chapter 7.) While squares do not appear in the transcripts I collected, boxes, which are another symbol, do appear.

The individuals who spoke the second and third "numeric" examples (above) were correct in stating that they had three days remaining. Perhaps there is something biological or spiritual that occurs three days before dying that makes this kind of precognition possible — or perhaps the similarities in these predictions were merely coincidental within this relatively small sample. The numbers eight and three reoccur in the transcripts. Eight has traditionally been associated with rebirth, change, and of course, the infinity symbol; three is associated with transformation and movement toward unity. Four marks completion or wholeness.

Hannah Roberts Brockow, who works in a hospice as a harp therapy practitioner, shared the following reflections with me about the number three:

I often hear these repetitive final phrases from the dying, and in my experience they, too, come in threes. Why three? It's a powerful number. The triangle is the strongest, most stable geometric shape. Three appears in religions all over the world in the distinctions of deities (Father, Son, Holy Spirit; Brahma, Vishnu, Shiva), and in the ways we pray to them (Sanctus, Sanctus, Sanctus; Kadosh, Kadosh, Kadosh; Namastasyei, Namastasyei, Namastasyei Namo Namaha). Nearly all sacred numbers in the world's religions are divided by three: 9, 33, 72, 108, to name a few. Jesus lived to be thirty-three. Ayurveda divides us into three doshas, and we these days divide ourselves into body, mind, and spirit.

Among the most prevalent exclamations are those that have to do with movement and motion:

Exclamations of Motion

"I've got to get off, get off! Off of this life. I'm dying. I'm dying."

"I am falling, I am falling, but I am not ready to go. They are getting ready to pick me up. When I fall, they are going to pick me up."

"It's time to get up, get up, get up…"

"I'm dying. I'm dying. The trains keep going by. The trains keep going by, but I can't get on. I've got the ticket. I have the ticket."

"She is coming for me. Coming for me. She said she is coming for me."

"I am coming, Mother!"

"The Jetta! The Jetta! The Jetta!"

"We have been able to continue the journey together. I want to continue together."

"Dad, I'm here! He is…is leaving, he's leaving, he's leaving."

"You are one stop from real hope, which means one stop from real hope."

"I am looking for the platform. Can someone show me where the platform is?"

"Going on a trip. Going on a trip."

"I have this beautiful dancing bear. I am dreaming of a dancing bear. He becomes an airplane. Then the airplane carries me away. Wouldn't it be sad if you didn't have your dancing bear?"

"Arms, two, three…Turn, two, three…Swing, two, three…Down, two, three…"

If these samples are a true reflection of the distribution of exclamations at the end of life, then this is a compelling revelation. It indicates that there is, indeed, a common experience of moving or going somewhere at the end of life. Perhaps this reflects the movement of consciousness as we shift dimensions. It is hard not to feel the power of movement evoked by these repetitive phrases, and by the themes of departure and motion, all of which are expressed even though the speaker may be completely restricted in movement.

Imagine the voice of a hypnotist guiding a client down a series of stairs, deepening a trance: "Take that first step, feeling the weight of your foot as it goes down. Now take that second step, feeling the weight of your foot sink even deeper. And that third step, heavier, heavier than before." Repetition can have the effect of moving us "down" somewhere even when, in actuality, there is little or no physical movement. It appears that repetition may be a kind of vehicle that can transport consciousness or even track its movement. Adam Eason, a hypnotherapist, explains, "Repetition is hypnotic, repetition is hypnotic, repetition is hypnotic."

A dramatic illustration of repetition and its association with shifting states of consciousness comes from Ben Radcliffe. Ben contacted me to share the unusual shifts in his language and perception that occurred after he suffered a traumatic accident, followed by a near-death experience while in a coma for twenty-seven days. When he emerged from the coma, he suddenly had new and powerful psychic abilities. He heard phrases "loop" in his head, and when he heard repeated phrases, they flagged psychic or intuitive knowledge. Ben learned to pay special attention when he heard these repeating segments, because he discovered they were likely to be precognitive.

Repetition appears in other intriguing ways. Ploce, a figure of speech that uses repetition, is common in poetry but not in everyday speech. However, it appears with some frequency at the end of life. In ploce, a word's meaning shifts when it's repeated, as does the part of speech it represents. A common example is "Charles is more English than the English," in which the word *English* occurs first as an adjective and then as a noun. The same sort of shift occurs in "Who will police the police?"

These phrases are perhaps more complex linguistic forms than a simple literal sentence such as "I am standing outside." Here are some examples of the fascinating use of ploce that appears in the transcripts I studied:

> "How much wider does this wider go?"
> "There is so much so in sorrow."
> "Here is the *here*; where is the *there*?"
> "God calling me home is not a clear call. God calls on
>   Monday, but I continue to live and breathe and be
>   alive."

And other interesting uses of repeated words or phrases emerge. For example, "I know that's not what's happening for me now, but I know what's happening is." This phrase, like many others I have heard over the years during my research, has the quality of a Zen koan, aimed at awakening both the speaker and the listener.

All these utterances shift the paradigms of language, as if to say, "A word's meaning in one context can become entirely different in another." The language is intriguing because, while we might expect some kind of deterioration in our use of language as our minds and bodies degrade, we actually see some very complex language — language that could be described as more complex than what we hear in the language of healthy people.

As a linguist, I cannot help but ask, "Why would we see such complex language at the end of life if our minds and consciousness are indeed waning?" The complex, and even poetic, language suggests to me that consciousness operates, and may even intensify in importance, as our bodies weaken. It is as if the language we associate with poetry and mysticism begins to predominate. This becomes even clearer in illustrations later in the book.

"I want to pull those down to earth somehow...I don't really know...No more earth binding...Little friends, I've got to bind some things together here."

"What is going on is the body of this report. Yeah, the report. If I understand it, up ahead of me is the body of this report. My report of what I have typed. My report to them is a report to you to say, 'Unfortunately we do not have a report. Inside from all that, the chair has no report.'"

Interestingly, the family members and beloveds who hear mysterious and poetic sentences such as these from their dying loved ones can often find meaning in their unusual constructions.

This was true for me when my father said, "There is so much so in sorrow." I knew immediately what he meant. This sentence expressed the intensity of our shared sorrow — indeed, there is so much sorrow, so much so. And what most intrigued me about this sentence is the repetition of the "so" that is in sorrow. How can a person be attuned to both the sound and the expressive quality of the words at a time when the body is disintegrating? I have seen this sophisticated use of repetition in the transcripts of many others, too.

One fascinating use of repetition appeared in the language of Elizabeth Mason's father as he stood at the threshold. Days before he died, he asked his wife for paper and a pencil, as if he had something very important to say. For an hour, he struggled to write, barely legibly, the sentence "The ghostly *ones* famed *one's* roles." Elizabeth explained:

It was difficult to read, but this is what jumped at me. He might have meant to write "framed," but "famed" could also fit. I believe my father was on the brink of passing over to another realm, one that we all will experience one day when we expire. My father was an MIT-trained scientist who taught at Brown University in the chemistry and engineering departments. He was not a religious man, nor did he share his spiritual thoughts and ideas, not with me, anyhow. He always had a scientific and pedantic explanation for everything, so this sentence that he wrote was quite out of character.

I truly believe that he was gaining insights as he neared his death, and that, like the good scientist he was, he wanted to record his experience. I do not think it was the morphine haze that influenced his words. I believe my father was communicating with those who had come before him, and he was experiencing a profound understanding of his entire life and how it played out. He had been influenced all along by others who were long dead, and these others had had a hand in the decisions my father made in life that led him to all that played out while he was on earth. That there are no coincidences in our lives was a dawning of deep truth. Other forces and energies influence us without our realizing it at the time. It all becomes clear at the end of our lives — and if we are open to it, sooner than that for many of us.

Some might say that Elizabeth read way too much into her father's sentence, but does that matter? What seems more important is that the language of our final days offers up rich meanings, much like poetry and mystical writing. The words connect us with those we love and seem to speak of a realm beyond this literal five-sense, three-dimensional world. As my seventeen-year-old said of her conversations with her grandfather, "It was like being in the company of souls."

Are these turns of phrase mere accidents? It does not seem that way to me. They, like poetry and mysticism, seem to be born of the spiritual realm. As we approach the threshold, often our language becomes more than ordinary and literal.

Here is another compelling illustration of repetition: "I am living between two places. Would like to make my *place mark* the other *place*. Re*mark*able." This sentence encapsulates the notion of being between locations. And when the speaker uses the word *mark* between "my place" and "other place," he seems to illustrate what he is explaining to us about being in a liminal place; the word *mark* is literally placed between the two "places." He tells us, and the language shows us, that this is "remarkable." At first glance, sentences like these may seem like nonsense, but as we look beyond the surface of language in later chapters, we will see more distinct patterns in the language. There is order in the language of the threshold, and the use of repetition is part of that order.

Repetition and Music

Studies indicate that repetition is a key feature of what we think of as musical. When people are exposed to melodies without repetition, they describe them as less musical than melodies that do have repetitive elements. Listen to the repetition of a musical phrase, and you'll find it is not hard to begin rocking back and forth and singing out loud. Music educator Elizabeth Hellmuth Margulis explains that "music takes place in time, but repetition beguilingly makes it knowable in the way of something outside of time. It enables us to 'look' at a passage as a whole, even while it's progressing moment by moment. But this changed perspective brought by repetition doesn't feel like holding a score and looking at a passage's notation as it progresses. Rather, it feels like a different way of inhabiting a passage — a different kind of orientation."

Repetition is closely related to music — and music is closely related to the part of human experience connected to mystical and spiritual experience. So just as metaphor has been demonstrated to engage both hemispheres of the brain, repetition in our language as we are dying may connect us to, and express our connection to, the part of human experience that exists outside of time.

In language, something called semantic satiation occurs when a word is repeated multiple times. When we hear a word the first or second time, we determine the meaning of the word — that is, we are engaged in recognizing its meaning. But when the word is repeated again, we respond to its tempo and pitch: we open up to the musical quality of language not accessible to us when we first hear it.

Christine Zagelow, a lifestyle coach in Washington State, shared her tender account of how she heard her mother's repetitive final words, which seemed to teeter at the edge of music.

> I stood next to her bed while I held her hand. I was on her left side. The IV machine feeding her a saline solution was beeping, and dripping continued inside the tube. Mom's head began turning from side to side, as if she were looking at something that was changing direction. Her eyes were closed, but I knew she was witnessing something beautiful and wonderful. I knew she was in a different space.
>
> She would say "Oh" and then look a different direction. Her facial expression changed from one form of softness to another. She continued to say "Oh,...oh," and each "oh" changed notes, like music in a song.

Repetition connects us to what is musical — that is, to tempo and pitch, which connect us more immediately to the nonverbal world, the world we can access only beyond literal language: "Oh, wow! Oh, wow! Oh, wow!"

Sustained Narrative and Repetition over Time

Repetition involves more than just single words and phrases: it also appears over time in the themes of some of the conversations that I studied. As mentioned earlier, the metaphors of the dying evolve over time. While some of the words may seem nonsensical when heard in isolation, they often form cohesive patterns over the course of days and weeks. For example, a conversation tracked over time may be something like the following one describing the "imaginary" companions of one woman's great-uncle:

March 10. "There's these guys playing poker, and they want me to be the fourth hand. I told them I don't want to play. I don't want to sit at their table and play."

March 15. "They're telling me I have to play, and I just don't want to. I don't want to be their fourth hand."

March 20. "I don't have no choice now, do I? They're bad folks, though. They are drinking and smoking. And I don't think I should be playing with them."

March 30. "It's okay. I don't have much choice anyway. I'll do what they say. I'll sit with them. I'll get out of my old chair here and sit with them."

When a transcript is studied over time, repetition of themes may emerge over days and weeks — and these repeated themes make their own kind of sense when examined over time rather than in isolation. A continuous narrative unfolds.

We saw examples of this when we looked at the metaphor of the journey and how metaphors evolve. It is not uncommon for someone to use a metaphor early in the dying process, such as "I need my suitcase," and then, as the dying process intensifies, to repeat the metaphor but change it in some way — for example, "Now that I have my suitcase, I need my passport. Where is my passport?"

What is remarkable is that the dying person seems to be engaged in a story unrelated to the world we know, and that it seems to endure and develop over days and weeks.

How often do you or I remember a story or theme that we began last week? Could you tell me about some idea or theme you articulated in a conversation ten days ago? Would you be able to progressively build upon that story or theme? Probably not. Our language and story lines are often rooted in the interactions we have with others from day to day, even minute to minute. While we may create sustained narratives when we write, it is rare to do so when we speak. When we write, we are able to capture and freeze our story lines and add to them; but in the utterances of the dying, certain symbols and story lines develop over days and weeks. How is it that the dying remember what they said two weeks ago and then continue on with the themes or stories from days or weeks past? Here are some examples that illustrate themes and narratives sustained over time:

Train

November 9. "I am concerned about the traffic going north. Now we are about to enter in…the…Now we have to get ready…communication north. By…not is by communication north…Yeah…The railroad…Yes, it should work smoothly like that…Yep…Lots of wreckage anterior lot of wreckage anterior…sorry to wake you…no water…I am so sorry…I am so sorry for the damage."

November 9, later in the day. "Dear, our connection in the north has made an error, has made a wrong turn. He may not correct for it. It looks like…our train which is going north will be in violation."

November 27. "Are you testing my engine. I am saying,

'Are you testing my engine?' Let me reverse if what I need to do is to reverse."

December 1. "I have thought of something under my control: the railroad stop."

The Report

November 5. "Report it. Let it be reported back along the… anybody have a reporting mechanism? It seems they have broken the law and will have…and in violation of the statute. Report it. Let it be reported back along the…anybody have a reporting mechanism?"

November 9. "We can, dear. What is going on is the body of this report — report — body of the report. Yeah, the report. If I understand it, up ahead of me is the body of this report. Sweetie, the occasion is over. My report of what I have typed…You don't have anything do you? My report to them is a report to you to say. Unfortunately we do not have a report…Inside from all that…the chair has no report."

November 9, later in the day. "What is going on is the body of this report. Yeah, the report. If I understand it, up ahead of me is the body of this report. My report of what I have typed. My report to them is a report to you to say. Unfortunately we do knothole a report. Inside from all that, the chair has no report. I would rather say, dear, that there is no report. Maybe that can be the report. What report finally got in the box?"

Doors

October 31. "Help me get in. Where? The front door."

November 5. "This is a major night because we are closing the door on Christmas. Well, my front door is partly your place."

November 6. "Well, you can join me in creeping back to our house. I am halfway between your place and mine. Yes, partly my place. Well…my front door…is partly your place. But you want to get to your place. In the long run…have to deal with your place and my place…This strip here…At some point, it will have to be closed, right? Maybe it wants to be closed. There is a tendency for us to close that space. Do you think there is? Yes, the possibility of area wanting closure."

In the following cases, loved ones shared with me the progression of a sustained narrative and the words spoken, but did not track the exact days.

Girl

"There's a girl wearing a blue skirt standing by my bed. She is watching me. We are feeling sad about it."

A few days later. "She is sitting closer. Why is she sitting so close to me?"

A few days later. "She is running down the hall now, but will be back soon."

Later still. "She is here now. Really close now."

The Champion

"I see the champion. He is here watching me."

"The soccer champion is back. This time he has his son with him. They are together now."

"They are in a big parade. I am watching them now."

"He's back. He does not have his son with him this time. What does he want with me? Why does he want me?"

Rain

"The rain is coming soon. The rain is coming closer now. Here it is. The storm."

While the repetition of words or phrases in the preceding remarks expresses increased intensity, the appearance of sustained narratives and repetition of specific themes or symbols represents an intensification in duration. Sustained narratives contain themes or symbols repeated over a period of time; and while the themes and symbols may not make sense when looked at in isolation, they evolve. Just as the near-death experience represents a narrative with certain landmarks, the narrative line in the stories of the dying at times also has repeated themes and clearly marked progressions.

As you look at the examples, you may notice that, while some of the sentences seem nonsensical or even poetic, they are still grammatical. That is, the sentences are structured like English; they are not disorganized or random. There seem to be principles of organization at play here; there are rules we may not fully understand, but they follow consistent patterns. The characteristic of following some of the rules of language and breaking others is an important distinction when we look at unintelligibility and nonsense in the following chapter.

You might also notice, in the samples above, the prevalence of the present tense. Final-words research in Germany confirms what I discovered during the Final Words Project: there is a greater focus on present time. The present tense often represents the unmarked form of a verb — that is, it describes a time that is neither past nor future. "I sing, she dances" can refer to an action taking place in the present, or it may be an abstract observation. The language of the dying appears to be slightly weighted toward the present. This, like repetition, intensifies their words. Often when we wish to bring special focus to or emphasize an experience, we recount it in the present tense, for example, "So I am just standing there, and this man comes up to me. He says, 'Give me your wallet.' I am so scared, I don't know what to say, but then…" Often, channels and mediums speak in the present tense, which can give great weight and meaning to the words spoken. The present tense also offers a sense of the "eternal now" — experience unmarked by time. Moody notes that when people recount their stories of near-death experiences, they often do so in present tense.

As noted earlier, the language of the dying is frequently intensified through the use of repetition and the common use of the present tense. Since repetition is one of the ways we add power to our language, it is not surprising that we use it in our dying days. The great English poet Alfred, Lord Tennyson, described the transcendent quality of repetition: "A kind of waking trance — this for lack of a better word — I have frequently had.…This has come upon me through repeating my own name to myself silently, till all at once, as it were out of the intensity of the consciousness of individuality, individuality itself seemed to dissolve and fade away into boundless being.…Have I not said the state is utterly beyond words?"

The repetition in the language of the dying expresses a number of themes, from agony to ecstasy. While this language may not sate our curiosity about what exists beyond the threshold, the use of repetition suggests that there are complex and systematic patterns at work in it. This kind of organization indicates that there may be much more than a disintegrating mind at play during our final days.

CHAPTER SIX

Nonsense or a New Sense?

Making Meaning out of
Unintelligible Language at the End of Life

Yes, I would like some scrambled eggs,
but where would you reappear?
— *Bill, Final Words Project participant*

L ike the patterns of repetition that emerge in the utterances of the dying, confusing and puzzling phrases, too, are common. It can be heartbreaking when the very people who once offered us comfort and connection no longer communicate in ways that we can understand.

My friend Lesly shared a story that resembled those I often heard from others: "My mom's losing it. Last night she told me, 'Look at all the guests with us! It's great to see everyone join us here for dinner!' But there was no one there. I don't get it. I feel like I am losing her even though she is still with me. She's just not making sense."

Sharon had this story:

My mom started talking about boxes — and needing to know where to put them. I did not know what boxes she was talking about. [Interestingly enough, as mentioned in chapter 3, boxes are one of the symbols that appear frequently in the Final Words Project stories and transcripts.]

And then I heard her jabbering away, and I could not understand. At first, it was terrifying to hear her. But as time progressed, her nonsense no longer frightened me, and I began to feel that the nonsense I heard was somehow helping her process her life in some way. I wish I knew exactly what was going on in her mind, but it was so hard to hear and make sense of her, and I had the distinct feeling that it was also a private reality.

It does seem that many of those who are crossing the threshold enter a private reality, and nonsense may track this extraordinary passage. As a linguist, I do not use the term *nonsense* pejoratively. I use it simply to refer to language that does not make sense in terms of what we know about our five-sense, three-dimensional world. We often use the word *nonsense* to disparage something, as in "That's total nonsense!" I am not speaking this way at all. Nonsense is a fascinating and dynamic language phenomenon and is as valid and as consistent in its structure, organization, and functions as intelligible language. Nonsense is, indeed, not of the senses as we know them. It is language that often appears outside of both normal experience and the usual narrative. Nonsense expressed by those on the threshold seems to come, as Sharon described, from a different place.

Babbling, Linguistic, and Situational Nonsense

Three kinds of nonsense are uttered by the dying: nonsense babbling, linguistic nonsense, and situational nonsense. But only two of these are found in the accounts and transcripts in my informal sample of data. The exact sounds and patterns of sounds that we sometimes hear in nonsense babbling at the end of life have gone almost completely undocumented. And only one participant in the Final Words Project was able to make any sense of the combinations of sounds and transcribe them. In a later chapter, I talk further about this kind of nonsense.

Linguistic nonsense refers to phrases and sentences that, in isolation, don't make sense to us. They have word combinations that are unintelligible. Some examples:

> "Tell Jack my modality is broken." (Modalities don't break.)
>
> "Introductory offer: store is closing for foods and goods run by the university." (The terms *introductory offer* and *closing for foods and goods* are contradictory — and a university does not usually offer foods and goods.)
>
> "There is so much so in sorrow." (*So* is not a noun. How can there be so much of it in *sorrow*?)
>
> "Water is most reliable." (Water generally is not associated with reliability, and it is not clear what the superlative *most* refers to.)

Interestingly, all the linguistic nonsense in my informal sample is grammatically and syntactically correct. This is called *categorical nonsense*. The sentences exhibit the correct grammar and syntax: the nouns are where they are supposed to be, the verbs are where they are supposed to be, but the categories do not fit together. For example, in the sentence "Tell Jack my modality is broken," the sentence sounds like English and all the parts are correctly placed. However, since modalities don't break, the sentence is a violation of what we know about the category "things that break." A "modality" is not among them.

In contrast, sentences that constitute situational nonsense make sense to us. The categories do fit together. For example, when my father said, "I am bringing the boxes to the art show," the sentence was perfectly intelligible. But it is nonsensical in context: he had no boxes in hand, and he had been walking down a busy street at midnight in his underwear. The reference to invisible guests at Lesly's dinner table is another example of situational nonsense, because although the language her mother used to describe the situation is linguistically correct, the sentences sound like nonsense given the context.

Here are some typical examples of situational nonsense:

> "There is a young woman standing at the foot of my bed." (Stated when there was no one in the room besides his daughter, who transcribed these words.)

> "Mom! Mom is here with me now." (The speaker's mother had died years earlier.)

> "It is so beautiful! It is so beautiful here!" (Stated while the speaker lay in an unattractive hospital room.)

> "Can you hear those bells ringing?" (No bells were ringing.)

> "I am in the green dimension." (Dimensions are not green.)

> "The white butterflies coming out of your mouth are so beautiful." (Butterflies do not come out of mouths.)

These sentences are linguistically meaningful but do not make sense in the context in which they are spoken.

Things Make No Sense without Context

A distinguishing characteristic of nonsense is that the context is missing. For example, if one hundred years ago someone had said, "The astronauts are going to the moon," the sentence would have been unintelligible. What are astronauts? How can anyone get to the moon? Many things that once would have seemed like nonsense are completely sensible today. Situational and linguistic nonsense are important in studying the language of the threshold because the language does not correspond to our current understanding and may hold hints of knowledge we do not yet have. As a matter of fact, a survey of many of the greatest discoveries in science is also a survey of concepts that were described at one time as complete nonsense. What looks like nonsense at any given point is often a harbinger of new frontiers.

It is interesting that the Final Words Project samples contain significantly less linguistic nonsense than situational nonsense. This may reflect our bias against linguistic nonsense. That is, most of us dismiss language that makes no sense to us, so it could be that people have not as freely transcribed, shared, recalled, or even noticed the linguistic nonsense that was uttered by loved ones in their last days.

Most people do not know how to respond to or even consider linguistic nonsense like "Introductory offer: store is closing for foods and goods run by the university" or "The sidewalks were in trouble and the bears were in trouble and I broke it up."

Finding Meaning in the Unintelligible

While nonsense uttered at the threshold is not well understood, some feel more comfortable with it than others do. Marie shared with me the fact that, as her husband was nearing death, he began to speak in gibberish. She simply spoke back to him, matching the rhythm, pace, and intonation of his words. One of his family members was so uncomfortable with this that she demanded of Marie, "Don't talk nonsense with him. Talk sense with him, so he will talk sense back." When Marie continued to speak her own "private language with her dying husband," the family member felt so threatened that she left the room. I have discovered that people react to nonsense in very different ways. For some, the emergence of nonsense threatens their sense of stability and safety — as does witnessing the death of someone they love. Loss, for most of us, is painfully unintelligible. However, from my interviews I've learned that many family members are able to move past the nonsense and find ways to connect, either by entering their loved one's new world or by simply nodding their heads kindly in love and agreement even though they may not understand anything that is said.

I asked Lesly, who was worried about her mother hallucinating guests at the dinner table, if she could enter into her mother's world and engage her in conversation. I suggested, for example, that she say, "Tell me all about the guests, Mom. I want to make sure I know who is here!" My friend started to cry. "I miss the conversations we used to have." A couple of weeks later she said, "I had been so focused on the loss of connection with her that I had not imagined we could connect again." Stephen Jones reflects, "When the dying speak, they need us to hear as well as feel. Simply dismissing their words as confused gibberish places too much responsibility on the speaker."

Situational nonsense offers opportunities to listen with our hearts and maintain our precious connections with people we love. The following example of situational nonsense from chaplain Cari Willis is a good example of how it offers opportunities to build bridges at the threshold with those we love:

> Years ago, I was able to spend the last several months of the life of my girlfriend Yukiko with her. The days and moments that I spent with her were filled with love, laughter, and wonder. But on one particular day as I was sitting quietly with one of Yukiko's very good friends, Yukiko sat up and told us: "Turn down that radio! I hate that music!" Her friend looked at me quite troubled, because the room, so quiet and peace-filled, seemed to us almost like sacred space.
>
> However, I went along with Yukiko and piped up and said, "Do you see the radio?"

After a few minutes went by, Yukiko said, "Yes."

"Well, see if you can find the knob to change the channel. You may have to turn it a time or two before you find
something you like."

Several minutes went by. The room was eerily silent now — we dared not speak or break the silence in
any way, shape, or form. Finally we heard from Yukiko a
loud "Ooooooooohhh, that is so much better. It worked.
I changed the channel. Thank you!" Yukiko's other friend
and I both broke out in laughter. We learned that day that,
while we could not hear the music in the room, to my
dying friend music was playing, and playing loudly — just
like she wanted it.

The radio in this example of situational nonsense illustrates, in
part, how I think of the nonsense of the threshold. It is like the
static we find between radio stations: nonsense may be what we
hear as we are tuning in to a different station. Since we, the living,
do not hear this station, the words from our loved ones sometimes
sound like gibberish.

Prepositional Nonsense

Because we do not know more about what happens when people
die, many of the nonsensical phrases we hear are situational nonsense. One form of situational nonsense that I consistently found
in the transcripts and other accounts of last words is what I call a
"prepositional shift." The words often make linguistic sense, but
they do not make sense in terms of what we currently know about
movement, bodies, direction, and space.

Prepositions are those small words that represent where we are
in space, such as: *in, out, on, up, over, through*. As people are dying,
they speak about location in disorienting ways. This language is

not unlike the language used to describe near-death experiences, in which people who lie motionless later speak of having been "out of" their bodies, passing "through" tunnels, and going "into" light, for example. Here are some examples in the language of the dying:

> "Help me down the rabbit hole."
>
> "I am living between two places...Would like to make my place mark the other place...Remarkable."
>
> "Hurry up, get me down...please...it's the end."
>
> "No. Wait a minute. You are one stop from real hope which means...one stop from real hope."
>
> "I want to pull those down to earth somehow...I don't really know...no more earth binding."
>
> "Help me lie down."
>
> "I got to go down there. I have to go down."
>
> "I've got to get down to earth. Help me."
>
> "That is who we are, where we are headed, okay, that's it."
>
> "I'm on top now — moving on top."
>
> "I am crossing up! Crossing up!"
>
> "I've got to get off, get off! Off of this life. I'm dying. I'm dying."
>
> "I am falling. I am falling but I am not ready to go. They are getting ready to pick me up. When I fall, they are going to pick me up."
>
> "It's time to get up, get up, get up..."
>
> "My body wants to go in one direction and the rest of me in another...this is not a situation of comfort."

Phrases like these are common and speak of orientation in space in unusual ways — up becomes down — backward and forward become confused — and the dying often ask us to somehow help them shift their position.

Sharon shared this account of a moment when her mother started complaining about her left leg:

"You're being asked to let go," I told my mom, just following my intuition. "To let go of your left side." •

"Yes," my mother said, "they say that's right. I'm trying to get out of this cage. I'm trying to get out of this cage. Now...my other leg."

The word *cage* here is evocative. When I asked Sharon what she thought her mother meant here, she talked about the cage of the physical body — of living here on earth. The metaphor strongly suggests a struggle for motion. Movement and metaphor work hand in hand in compelling ways in the following account as well: "Daddy-o was asking me to push him backwards....His bed is against the wall, so I told him that felt difficult....He looked so sad....I asked him why he wanted me to push him backwards,... and he said, 'Because everything that is important to me is behind me.'"

This transcription makes references to choosing the right direction:

I am dying, you know. I know I am dying. My family doesn't like me to say it. And it used to make me really sad. But now I think it's funny. Not everybody wants to hear about it, my dying. I know I will die from this. They want to do more procedures, but it is all over. My family doesn't like me to talk like this. Sometimes the problem is I don't know my left from right. It's like a game. Which direction should I go? And when I go there, I find out it was the wrong direction or I don't know why I went there.

These examples articulate the sense of changing motion and disorientation. And in some cases, there are metaphors closely associated with movement. At first glance, it could appear that they reflect disorientation caused by medications or deterioration of certain parts of the brain. However, other examples of the language of the threshold indicate that much more may be going on.

Physician Tony Ciccoria, who had a near-death experience when he was hit by lightning, demonstrates prepositional shift when he speaks about his experience: "The force of the lightning blast threw my body backwards like a rag doll. Despite the stunning physical trauma, I realized something strange and inexplicable was happening. *As my body was blown backwards, I felt 'me' move forward* instead. Yet, I seemed also to stand motionless and bewildered staring at the phone dangling in front of me. Nothing made sense."

Dr. Ciccoria speaks paradoxically about his movement: his physical body went backward, and yet he had a sense that something was moving forward. What was that something? Notice the same thing in a description recorded in Kenneth Ring and Sharon Cooper's landmark research into near-death experiences of the blind:

> The body that was on the bed was absolutely still and did not have any movement. I felt that it was something that must have come out of me…[when I] drifted up to the ceiling. Something that was left of me would be still on the bed. For a very brief moment I wondered why I felt like I was sort of two people at the same time. I saw one part of me absolutely still as if being ready to be detained, and yet there was a very integral important part of me that was about to float up beyond the ceiling to this new realm wherever it might have been.

This description by a blind person is compelling for a number of reasons. The first, of course, is that he makes many visual descriptions even though he is blind. Ring and Cooper's research documents the fact that 80 percent of their blind participants, most of them blind from birth, were able to see during their near-death experiences. Ring and Cooper's example, like many other accounts, also speaks in interesting ways about motion and movement. Descriptions found in research about near-death experiences are closely related to the language that emerges at the threshold.

A hospice worker nicknamed "Zany Cat" explained:

> Even though I don't believe in heaven, you have to wonder if indeed it exists, or if somehow we are programmed to think it does. George Carlin, the comedian, said, "Why is it people never say, 'I think he's down there now, smiling up at us'? We are always saying things like: 'My dad's smiling down at me here on earth.' We never hear, 'My dad's screaming up at us.' Why do we imagine that we are always going up when we die?" See, I don't believe in heaven, but I have to wonder why our words are like that. I have noticed that at least 20 percent of the time I do hear something about patients talking about going up or over. There is reference to moving, although they are right there in beds.

A hospice nurse from Trinidad described to me such references to movement this way: "In my country, the nonsense that is spoken by the dying is called 'traveling.' We believe that these nonsense words are part of the process of the soul leaving, going upward to the Great Beyond."

Nonsense is associated with language that falls outside the ordinary, literal narrative of our lives. People under stress talk nonsense as if to flag the critical quality of their state. Nonsense announces, "The words I use now show you that I am not in an ordinary state of consciousness... Something is shifting."

Extreme stress makes people talk nonsense. Soldiers, for example, sometimes talk incoherently when rescued from horrific battles in which they narrowly avoided death or life-threatening injury. This is also true of people who have been involved in other terrifying events. One explanation I've heard from medical experts is that when something overwhelming happens to us, it is as if our brain short-circuits. It is as if the vast unintelligibility of the experience gets translated into unintelligible language. This suggests that, as we approach death, and we contemplate the overwhelming reality of death, we become desperate to avoid it. In such circumstances, nonsense reflects a last-ditch attempt at escape. Why is this so? It appears that our minds may be programmed to use nonsense as an escape route — and the mystery is this: What are we escaping to, and how is nonsense the pathway out?

As people die, their language expresses a sense of movement, even though we often see before us the stillness of a body approaching death. My father's words were typical of what I heard from others. "Help me down from here," he said as he lay on his bed a few days before dying. I imagine he may have been experiencing what near-death experiencers describe as leaving their bodies and ascending upward, only to look down at themselves on the earth below. This in itself is paradoxical: How can you be motionless and moving upward at the same time? Since this sense of motion also appears in the language of the NDE, perhaps something is going on in the subjective experience of being at the threshold. The dying seem to be, in the words of the poet Rumi, "going back and forth across the doorsill where the two worlds touch."

When we imagine a person lying completely still and later describing having had an experience filled with motion, it offers the possibility that as we die, we enter a realm in which dual realities can coexist. Or the possibility that the reality we know through the five senses is giving way to something entirely new, something our literal language cannot grasp.

You may recall paradoxical statements like these from chapter 2 made by people who had near-death experiences:

> "I felt more alive when I was dead than when I was living."
>
> "I understood everything everyone said, but not a word was spoken."
>
> "I left my body and traveled through the galaxies, all while I was lying motionless in bed."

The nonsense in the language of the dying, like that of the language of the NDE, does not express the world as we know it. So much of the language is paradoxical. A few examples from the Final Words Project include:

> "*Introductory* offer: store is *closing* for foods and goods."
>
> "I am going *up* so I can go *down*."
>
> "No, but if *you don't and you do, then you do*."
>
> "Grant me *half a full* measure of it."
>
> "I don't think there is progress in *winning and losing* again."

Prepositional nonsense expresses and reflects paradox: up is down and down is up. In the same way, the language of self-contradiction is unlike our usual language. These utterances seem closely related to the remarkable paradoxes we hear described by near-death experiencers, such as "I was able to see although I am blind."

In our five-sense, three-dimensional reality, we cannot be blind and see — or even consider that polar-opposite concepts could coexist. But we have seen in the NDE research of Ring and Cooper, for example, that the blind report seeing in moments when they are clinically dead — and we have heard from hundreds of near-death experiencers about paradoxical events that are difficult to put into literal, ordinary language. This kind of paradoxical language is more prevalent among dying people than among healthy people. This is true of hybrid nonsense as well.

Hybrid Nonsense

That dual realities might coexist is seen in a pattern that I call hybrid nonsense, which occurs frequently in the language of the threshold. One part of the sentence is grounded in what is perceptible; another part isn't. It is as if the speaker has one foot here in this dimension and one foot in a world we do not see.

> "Get me my checkbook since I have to pay to get in."
>
> "I need my pearls for the dance tonight." (There is no dance.)
>
> "Please massage my feet so I can get down into the rabbit hole." (The speaker's girlfriend is massaging his feet while he lies on a hospital bed. There are no holes.)
>
> "Get my camera. I need to take a picture of this." (There is nothing to take a picture of.)
>
> "They left the ladders, but the ladders are too short to go up there." (The speaker is referring to ladders outside her bedroom window.)
>
> "Please leave some money and baby clothes on my bed. I will need them in heaven when I have my baby." (The speaker is a thirteen-year-old girl dying of cancer.)
>
> "I better get dressed now. I need to go home."
>
> "Get me scissors so I can cut this out of here."
>
> "Help me thread this pencil to the other side."

Cari Rush Willis, who has sat at the bedside of almost two hundred dying people, including some on death row, said:

I always say that people at the end of their lives have one foot in heaven and one foot on earth. Folks who are dying can see things I cannot. To deny their reality is a huge mistake. It is so important that anyone sitting at the bedside of someone who is dying be willing to hear and affirm the person's reality. Stay silent and be present. I even cry with the guys in the hospice units in prison. I gave up on all I learned about not crying. I just think a life is worth crying over — most of them have not had their lives cried over.

One minister shared the story of a congregant at the end of life who began speaking of the big party she was getting ready to attend. She asked for a piece of paper to write down the names of the attendees. Her son, who was also present, asked to see the list, curious about what his mother had in mind. All those whose names were written down were family members and friends who had passed away. Mixing the metaphor of the dance with the practical and grounded realities of needing a pen and paper, this woman prepared for dying. This is a typical example of hybrid nonsense.

In the last two weeks of my father's life, he moved in and out of periods of extreme lucidity and of deconstruction of the world he knew and we shared, which revealed itself particularly in his language. At moments, he spoke of the reality we had in common: "Bring me a little water, please, dear." But he also referred to a place he called the "green dimension." He spoke of the "interim spaces of poems" and the degrees of "so" in the word "sorrow." He told me that poems were a form of prayer and then reminded my mother that she would need to bring his oxygen tent (there was none, actually) for their trip to Las Vegas (which had been canceled months earlier). He did not have Alzheimer's disease or another form of dementia; these fluctuations in consciousness came from a lucid mind.

Through his language, I could enter into his process of dying, until the moment of his death, when he took the hand of my mother, his wife of fifty-four years, and said a simple "Thank you, thank you." There appeared to be little or no relationship between his lucidity and his medications. The shifts in consciousness and language appeared to have a timing of their own.

A coma survivor interviewed by Madelaine Lawrence described what it had been like for her to move between states of consciousness:

> The next thing I remember was my children. I remember my one son calling me, "Mom, Mom," he kept saying. "If you can hear me, move your toe."...I tried to move my toe...But then I was gone again...I would go into unconsciousness. It wasn't just nothing. It was a dark, dark, warm place. It didn't frighten me — but it was always very dark — just darkness and warmth.

Dr. Martha Jo Atkins shared an account with me that has the same feeling of moving between states of being or, possibly, dimensions:

> What came to him close to death was the ocean and the beach, and those two just started merging into one...kind of right where the wave comes up and then goes out. So the beach and the ocean meshed into one and held him. And he just melted away into that. He did visit the ocean a lot, and it was very important to him, so it made sense.

Nonsense and Transcendent Experience

Nonsense appears in a variety of contexts, including mystical and spiritual traditions in which gibberish is associated with opening doors to new dimensions. We find the use of linguistic nonsense in chanting, spells, and incantations, for example. Nonsense is often associated with opening portals to new worlds and giving us a chance to stand between them. As children we learn that nonsense words like *shazam* and *abracadabra* can move mountains or take us to new worlds. If you have the right word, you can open doors. Spells and incantations are often composed of nonsensical words that promise us access to powers outside our normal lives.

Nonsensical language is language that falls outside our usual experience or earthly powers — and this has been true over the centuries and around the world. Dr. Will Taegel, author of *The Mother Tongue*, reflected in an email to me: "The pursuit of nonsense to enter realms impervious to rational penetration has been present in the wisdom and shamanic traditions in time immemorial. Drumming, drugs, chanting, dancing, strenuous physical orders, inebriation of all sorts have been utilized to take people out of normal reality into extraordinary reality across virtually all human cultures. There is something about nonsense that helps us make sense of our unfathomable lives." Taegel explained that shamans over time have told us, "We cross over to the other side by the power of our nonsensical songs."

The American psychologist William James observed that self-contradictory expressions like "dazzling obscurity," "whispering silence," "teeming desert," and "the Soundless Sound" are common in the writings of mystics. Apparently, prosaic language is inadequate for describing the transcendent level of consciousness. Raymond Moody suggests, "We delight in nonsense because it short-circuits the brain by bypassing the rational mind."

Moody believes that nonsense — what Will Taegel calls "transsense" — is the intermediary language between the two worlds of acquired language and a universal telepathic language that seems to exist in the realm of the afterlife, as explained by near-death experiencers. That nonverbal telepathic realm is the realm of the ineffable that mystics, including Buddhist teachers, speak about.

Zen Buddhists use nonsense as a means of spiritual enlightenment. Zen masters present unanswerable questions, known as koans, to students. Some koans are nonsense questions: "Does a dog have Buddha nature or not?" and "Two hands clap and there is a sound. What is the sound of one hand?" The questions are designed to move students away from understanding life only in a logical way and to connect them with something that is ineffable, not of the ordinary world as we know it. Koans invite us to enter into another way of thinking, and they seem to baffle our minds while bringing us to a greater understanding.

Milton Erikson, a world-renowned hypnotherapist, often used nonsense to distract and confuse a client's conscious mind when he wanted to make a hypnotic suggestion. He understood that nonsense acts as a bridge to another state of consciousness, another way of thinking.

Nonsense syllables have been attributed directly to God by those who speak in tongues. Referred to as glossolalia, speaking in tongues happens during periods of religious ecstasy, and some claim it is the holy spirit talking through congregants. Linguistic research, however, indicates that the phonological and prosodic patterns found in glossolalia mimic the patterns of the native language of its speakers — and these patterns shift with different languages. This tells us that the language itself is not a universal Divine language; however, the ecstatic experiences of its speakers appear to be universal. Preliminary research shows that glossolalia engages the regions of the brain associated with mystical experience and music.

So, even though glossolalia is not a unique language, the nonsense syllables of glossolalia alter our consciousness. This has been documented through the use of brain scans. Researchers compared brain scans of individuals doing a common language task, such as reading aloud, with brain scans of individuals speaking in tongues. The parts of the brain activated during speaking in tongues are more closely connected to the regions activated during the non-verbal states of mystical or spiritual trance than to the centers associated with speech and language. Meaningless speech appears to both create and reflect extraordinary altered states of consciousness. There may even be evidence of "magical language" — that is, language designed to help us shift dimensions, as is found in glossolalia, spells, incantations, and shamans' songs.

Enlightenment Changes Your Brain

Andrew Newberg and Mark Robert Waldman have done extensive research into how altered and transcendent states correlate with brain function. They describe having observed immediate decline in activity in the language areas of the frontal lobes of Pentecostal participants speaking in tongues. They explain, "Normally when you talk and listen to others, the communication centers in your brain turn on, but when a person begins speaking in tongues, these areas shut down." Similar changes in brain activity occur during trance states in shamans and mediums. Newberg and Waldman say that these neurological changes create the pathways to enlightenment experiences.

On his website, Eben Alexander shares some interesting research on hallucinogens and the brain that supports Newberg and Waldman's findings and sheds light on the language used at the end of life. Research at Imperial College in London in 2012 revealed that among people under the influence of psilocybin, those whose psychedelic experiences were most profound had "greatly diminished" activity in the "major connection regions" of the brain. Alexander also references a Brazilian study completed in 2015 that researched the effects of ayahuasca and confirmed a decrease in activity throughout an important region of the brain called the default-mode network. Alexander cites yet another study at Imperial College, this one on the effects of LSD on the brain, which found that a diminished integrity of certain regions of the brain seemed to be associated with extraordinary states of consciousness.

About his coma and near-death experience, Alexander writes:

> As my neocortex was destroyed by the invading bacteria, my conscious awareness greatly *expanded* to levels unprecedented in my normal waking experiences of my entire life. That shocking reality nagged at me especially in the early months after my coma, at a time [when] I was trying to explain the whole experience as a vast hallucinatory trick of the dying brain (defaulting to my pre-coma reductive materialistic scientific beliefs, honed by several decades working as a neurosurgeon).
>
> My doctors knew from the medical evidence in my case that my neocortex was far too damaged to be supporting any mode of robust conscious experience, including any elaborate hallucinations, drug effects or dream states. After extensive review with some of the doctors who cared for me, and with several interested colleagues in neurosurgery, it became apparent that that ultra-reality occurred because the experience was real, although it did not occur anywhere in our 4-dimensional space-time of the observable physical universe.

I asked Andrew Newberg if it might be possible that, as we begin dying and the speech centers associated with language diminish, we have increasing experiences of mystical states like those described by Eben Alexander. These states of mind may also be associated with the nonsense that we hear. Newberg said he thought it is very possible that as we die, brain function associated with logic and reason — and with the production of purposeful speech —

does, indeed, shut down. This could cause, for the dying person, a number of experiences that are mystical in quality and rich in unintelligible speech.

This is what intrigues me. If it were merely nonsense, all kinds of nonsense, that appeared as we die, then I would easily concede that these utterances merely reflect declining brain function. However, as I have shown, the language seems to cluster around certain themes and patterns of nonsense. Nonsense is language that does not make sense in our usual five-sense, three-dimensional reality. However it does have its own rules. It is actually a more complex form of language than literal intelligible language, since it is defined only by the rules it is breaking. Nonsense is built upon the meanings of "sensical" language. So, from a linguistic point of view, we actually see more complex language in the days when we would expect disintegration of language function. That is, we use, interestingly enough, a preponderance of complex language forms as we approach death, such as the hybrid and paradoxical constructions discussed in this chapter, as well as the metaphoric language illustrated in earlier chapters. Each type of nonsense respects some rules of language and breaks others — and it appears that human beings are preprogrammed not only for sense-making language but also for nonsense.

There are many kinds of nonsense. Dr. Raymond Moody, in his unpublished book "Making Sense of Nonsense," explains that he has identified seventy types, and he offers examples of many of these. The transcript that I studied shows that most of them center on a handful of particular patterns — some of which I have introduced already, and others that I will share in chapter 8. I understand that my data set is not rigorous and is relatively small. But the patterns are intriguing: Why do we find such a clustering of paradoxical and hybrid utterances? Why in all of the utterances that I have collected does the nonsense retain coherent grammar and syntax? The answers may be found in the pages ahead.

CHAPTER SEVEN

Words between the Worlds

Descriptions of Visions and Visitations before Dying

He said just a few words: "Hallelujah! My wife!"
He had a big smile on his face. And I don't remember
hearing anything else from him again.
— *Mark, Final Words Project participant*

In the previous chapter, we looked at the degree to which context determines whether something makes sense to us. That is, if certain information is missing or is not perceived by the listener, then certain utterances or ideas are unintelligible. The following story from hospice volunteer Malynda Cress is a good example: "What's it going to be like when I die?" a patient asked her. "Tell me about the birds. What happens to them when they die?" Malynda was puzzled. "The patient was curious about the mechanics of dying — his and birds' [dying], and other odd combinations. I wanted to understand more about this man, so I went to his chart. There, it was written: air force pilot, World War II. He had also been involved in the mechanics of both cars and camping. Mechanics had been a theme throughout his adult life. Knowing the mechanics of dying, for himself and the birds, made far more sense then." Once Malynda had access to the context, she had a greater understanding.

Nonreferential Language

As we die, we may make references that are unclear to the living. This is called low-referential, or nonreferential, language. Dying individuals refer to people, places, or objects not apparent to their beloveds. Subject pronouns such as *it* and *this*, in which the referent is ambiguous, are common in transcripts and accounts.

My father's final words to his typist a day before he died were "*This* is very interesting, Alice. I've never done *this* before." What was this enigmatic "this"? The word *this* echoed in my thoughts as I contemplated why he never said, "Dying is very interesting. I have never died before." Could it be that the word is unmentionable, too difficult for our minds to grasp in those final moments, or could it be that nobody dies? Was my father having an experience that could not be put into words — a "this" for which there is no language — like the ineffable experiences of those who survive near death? What was the *this* he was experiencing? I was intrigued by the lack of referent, curious about what might lie behind that mysterious "this." The nonreferential pronouns *it* and *this* (and a few other terms) leave the listener wondering, as in the following examples:

> "*It* is very beautiful over there." (What exactly is beautiful, and where is "there"?)
>
> "Too bad I cannot tell you of all of *this*." (What is "this"?)
>
> "*It's* not what you think." (What is it, then?)
>
> "My vocabulary did *this* to me" (from poet Jack Spicer).
>
> "Lots of people have *this*…"
>
> "*It's* all in one piece…*It's* all in once piece…What you see in different pieces…*it's* all in one piece."
>
> "Too bad I cannot tell *of all* I have seen.
>
> "I know *that's* not what's happening for me now, but I know *what's* happening is…"

"I can't tell you about *it*."

"You will find out later." (About what?)

"There is nothing they can do for *this*."

The lack of referents implies there are things that the speaker cannot or may not explain. This gives a general feeling that what the speaker is experiencing is either indescribable or may not be communicated. It is not clear what cannot be told, who is not allowed to be told, or why certain details or references are withheld.

These qualities are also consistent with the experiences of near-death experiencers who explain that certain information is being withheld until they cross the last frontier of death. Many describe how they were instructed or shown that certain things cannot be shared or revealed to them until they die completely and finally. Typical of the descriptions of near-death survivors is that of Shawna Ristic: "There was an understanding that there was this barrier — a frontier to be crossed — and it was decided that I was not going to cross over it. What lay beyond it remained a secret."

References to life being an illusion also emerge in the accounts and transcripts with the same kind of nonreferential speech:

"*It is* all a hoax. Just an illusion." (Italics added; Roger Ebert's well-documented last words. What is a hoax?)

"Today early the Lord told me in representation." (What did he tell you?)

"Amazing! I don't believe *it*! *These* are for real?" (What do "it" and "these" refer to?)

This typical description from a near-death experiencer may shed light on what the dying might be witnessing: "The light showed me the world is an illusion. All I remember about this is looking down…and thinking, 'My God, it's not real, it's not real.' It's as if all material things were just props for our souls, including our bodies." It may be that the words we hear from the dying come from a sea of ineffable metaphysical experience. And we, the living, are merely witnesses to language at the tip of the iceberg.

One utterance I received through the Final Words website is "I miss myself," which made me think of my aunt's final words a few months earlier. "The pronoun is all wrong," my aunt said as she was approaching the end of her life. I wish now that I could have asked her, "What pronoun?" or "Which *is* the right one?" Perhaps she was referring to the pronoun *I* — saying that somehow *I* is not the right pronoun for who we are as we cross the threshold. Perhaps as mystics and spiritual teachers have told us across time, there really is no "I" — in the same way that others have referred to this life as being simply an illusion.

Of all the nonreferential language that people use at the threshold, the most common is language referring to people or places unseen by the living. The dying speak of visitors of all kinds. Here are some typical examples:

Visions of Crowds

"Who are all those people out there?"

"There are so many people in here. I don't have time to talk to all these people."

"My father died on a Friday morning. He spent the entire Wednesday before that talking, sometimes out loud and sometimes muttering under his breath to a variety of people he had known throughout his life. It was the most amazing thing I have ever seen."

Visions of a crowd have also been reported through the eyes of children and can bring comfort to their parents in the most tragic of circumstances. A young mother shares her daughter's last words:

I was twenty-eight and had a very ill, six-and-a-half-year-old, wonderful daughter who had fibrosarcoma of the jaw (which young children rarely get). It had grown into a huge tumor on the outside of her lovely face and had also grown into a fairly large tumor inside her mouth. She awoke at 6:30 AM on a Monday morning, and I noticed her little fingernails had turned blue. I knew the ending was near.

I took her into my mom's kitchen to give her some cold orange juice, since she enjoyed this, and I walked around the little kitchen table and leaned against my mom's sink to watch my young daughter drink her juice. All of a sudden, she looked up at me and pointed near me and asked, "Who are all those people standing there, Mommy?" I first thought perhaps I had not heard her correctly, so I asked her what she had just said. She repeated to me, "Who are all those people standing there, Mommy?" And I somehow knew "they" had come to help her over (no, I am not religious, spiritual, if you will). I walked around the table to pick her up, and she jerked and went into a coma, from which she did not recover. She died in the local hospital just hours later. Of course, I will never forget this moment, ever…and it has given me some peace.

Reports of visitations in preparation for a journey are consistent with all the metaphors of travel discussed in chapter 4. Perhaps the dead — or our vivid memories of them — do indeed come to "take us away."

The Arrival of Deceased Loved Ones

While dying people may describe seeing groups of people, they most commonly identify a loved one, usually a family member, as having come to bring them "home" or take them somewhere.

This example from Donna is typical: "It was as if my dad were speaking to my mom — who had died ten years earlier — by phone, and I heard only his end of the telephone call. He was so excited and happy. It was hard to believe that it was just imagination. Something very real seemed to be going on."

The reunions are often joyous. They not only offer comfort to those who are dying but also can reassure those who are nearby and who understand what is going on and are not afraid. While these "take-away figures" remain unseen by us, they are often vivid to those who do see them. "Don't you see him there? There he is!" one sixty-eight-year-old mother exclaimed to her daughter, pointing to the younger woman's father, who had died ten years earlier. "Here's Mom, I have to go now" was a phrase I heard from several people. The following are some other examples I recorded:

> "I was in the other room, and I heard my mother talking and talking. I came to her and asked who she was speaking to. 'I am talking to your father!' she said. My dad had died eight years earlier. She seemed so happy. 'I feel so much more calm now,' she explained, 'much better now.'"

> "My mom was speaking to my stepdad, who had died a few years earlier. She was telling me how much better she felt when she saw him."

> "I had a family member who went into cardiac arrest. She survived for a time afterward. She talked about how she saw her dad, our grandmother, and aunts, and how they were all standing there, waiting on her. She said that she recalled telling them she was not ready, but that she told them she missed them and loved them."

Dorothy explained to me that her sixty-six-year-old husband, a Vietnam veteran, died after a long struggle with the dilatation effects of Agent Orange. At his final dinner, he asked her about the woman who had been there all day. She replied that they had been alone. Because he was heavily medicated, he had often had vivid dreams, and Dorothy simply thought this was another one. He persisted, saying that she had been there for a long time, that she was someone he knew well, but he couldn't remember her name. (He was terrible with names.) He got up from the table, took his plate to the kitchen, kissed Dorothy (not something he did normally after a meal), and went to her room for a nap from which he never awoke. She told me, "I wish now that I had asked him questions instead of dismissing it. It comforts me to think that someone he loved very much came to take him home."

If you hear a loved one begin to speak of or with a deceased friend or family member, you can ask questions and lean into that moment fully, for it may be a signal that death is near, as in the following example. "It began with my mother telling me about a young girl dying, who, on her deathbed, had seen visions of angels and relatives who had passed. For a moment the girl talked to them, and then she told the people at her bedside not to worry about her, that she would have to go now. And then she passed."

One public account of a predeath vision followed comedian Sam Kinison's death in a head-on collision in 2009. Carl LaBove, Kinison's best friend, was traveling in a van behind him when the accident occurred. The story was published in several places, including the *New York Times*. This report comes from Paul Luvera:

At first it looked like there were no serious injuries to Kinison, but within minutes he suddenly said to no one in particular: "I don't want to die. I don't want to die." LaBove later said [that] "it was as if he was having a conversation, talking to some unseen somebody else," some unseen person. "Then there was a pause as if Kinison was listening to the other person speak. Then he asked, "But why?" and after another pause LaBove heard him clearly say: "Okay, Okay, Okay." LaBove said: "The last 'Okay' was so soft and at peace... Whatever voice was talking to him gave him the right answer and he just relaxed with it. He said it so sweet, like he was talking to someone he loved.

Angels and Religious Figures

As mentioned in the introduction, one of the many phrases that compelled my interest in final words was one spoken by my atheist father a short time before he died. As he neared death, he announced, "The angel said 'Enough... That's it... enough... enough... no one's to blame... go now...'" This was from a man who never spoke about angels — if anything, he ridiculed the whole idea and believed strongly that death was final. However, three days later, as the angels told him, it was enough, and my father passed away. How was it that my skeptical father saw angels? How did he know that he would be dying in three days?

While visions of the predeceased are the most common visions mentioned in the accounts and transcripts, there were also references to angels and religious figures. For example, one person reported, "My grandmother, who was a religious woman, told me she saw a yellow bus filled with angels, and they were getting ready to open the door." Another person said of a dying individual, "She even described Jesus fully, until the point it gave me chills."

A retired hospice nurse described one of her patients in his last moments:

I was holding him up in his hospital bed so he could get air better. He looked up toward the ceiling and said, "Do you see them?" I said, "No sir. Tell me what you are seeing." He raised his right arm and pointed up, saying, "There are angels all along the right and over there on the left. I have to go now." He called out to his wife, who was crying in the kitchen. "Carol, I have to go now. I love you. I'll see you again." Then he again raised his right arm toward the ceiling and said, "My Lord, my God." And he fell back against me. He was gone.

Music, Bells, Chimes

There were also descriptions of beautiful music and sounds in the accounts people shared with me:

My mother said there was music: "It is the most beautiful thing I have ever heard." I reassured her it must be angels. I had the sad gut feeling this would be our last time together in this lifetime. I could see her face light up, and that it was drawn to this music she heard. I felt compelled to tell her that I was okay and that everyone was going to be okay, giving her permission to go. I looked back as I left that night and saw her sit up in the bed and wave good-bye. She passed away that night. Eighteen years have passed, and I still can't keep a dry eye with this memory.

My mother was in a palliative care ward. During my visit, she was very talkative and mentally stable. She just stopped speaking, gazed up at the corner of the room, and asked me, "Do you hear that music? It is so beautiful!" I replied, "No, Mom I can't. What are you talking about?"

I have witnessed three passings: my grandfather, my mother-in-law, and my father. All three spoke of hearing beautiful music that no one else could hear. Grandpa spoke of an angel singing, my mother-in-law heard Native American ceremonial music, and Dad could not speak well. He said the word *music*, closed his eyes, and moved his head to a melody that I did not hear. All three passed within hours [of hearing the music].

Animals, Young Children, and Landscapes

Among the less common visions described by dying people are those that feature animals, children, and landscapes. A few people referred to seeing both deceased pets and deceased animals that were unfamiliar but reassuring to the dying person. I encountered references to dogs, cats, and butterflies.

Butterflies often appear as a symbol of the transformative power of death as we shed the cocoon of our bodies for the free flight of the spirit. They function as a symbol of hope and immortality in a variety of contexts — including in one of the most dispiriting environments imaginable. At Majdanek, a Nazi German concentration camp built in Poland, hundreds of butterflies were scratched onto the walls of the children's barracks with fingernails and pebbles.

The juxtaposition of great scenes of beauty and moments of loss and despair occur often at the threshold. At times, scenes of indescribable landscapes appear before the dying. The nonreferential *it's* appears in these descriptions, too, as in "It's so beautiful." Rarely do I see vivid descriptions of the landscapes that dying people witnessed, but there is wonder. My father talked about the "green dimension," which was never really clear to me. One man described his grandfather's experience: "He said very happily, as if in awe: 'Look, pretty flowers!'" Lucia shared her father's description of a beautiful forest that stretched across the hospital wall, with a door on either side of the landscape. She related how he had struggled to know which door he should enter: he spoke to his daughters in their native language, Spanish, saying, "'Not that door...open the other one.' And then finally my sister said, 'It's okay, it's okay...,' and he finally died."

Men in Black

The image of men in black emerged a few times in the Final Words Project interviews and transcripts, as in this example:

> All week she had been talking about these men in black suits standing in her room. Well, I went to assist the other staff in turning her, and before we did so, she said, "Don't turn me. Those men are waiting for me." We asked her why they were there and what they wanted. She stated, "They want to take me." We tried to adjust her without completely turning her, and she was fine. Then hours later, she was turned and took her last breath.

Madelaine Lawrence reports that while not as prominent as other deathbed visions, the Grim Reaper and other dark images appeared in her research into end-of-life and near-death visions. They do not seem to be as prominent, but they do exist. For example, a woman whose husband

> was dying from end-stage liver cancer reports her husband saw shadow people at the edge of his room. In his case he said there were 12 to 20 of them. He asked her to take a trip, hoping they would cast off the shadow figures. He again saw them in the hotel at which they were staying. They moved to a relative's house but still the shadow figures found them. The husband could not tell if they were good or bad entities, but he knew he was afraid of them.

This account given to me by Christine Zagelow is filled with images of smoke, the unseen, forgiveness, and a mysterious reference to something that cannot yet be shared:

She said, "Where is the smoke coming from?" I didn't see any smoke. She began to grab at the air in front of her. I asked what she was doing, and she said she was trying to catch the sparks of light that were in the smoke. Then she began saying, "The smoke, the smoke, can't you see the smoke? Smoke is everywhere." Her voice seemed different, so very clear, yet different. She said her insides were hot, and it felt like the smoke was in her blood. I thought maybe her cancer was being burned out of her, leaving her clear of the dis-at-ease she was having. The burning seemed to work itself out. She then began to tell me a vision she could see just over the television set.

[In this vision] a man stood in front of the church wearing a cook's hat. I asked her if she thought it was Grandpa (her father), and she said she couldn't tell. Then my mom said, "You know, I can't see you anymore, the room is very dark." Mom turned to me and said I was the only thing she could see, that she had never seen me looking so beautiful. She said, "You are completely surrounded by white lights. They are the brightest lights I have ever seen. You absolutely glow." We said how much we loved each other. She put her hands in front of her head and began making the shape of a square or circle as if to capture something. I asked her what she was doing, and she tried to explain as her words became unclear. She swayed her hands and said, "I'll tell you later."

Of all end-of-life communications, deathbed visions have been the most widely studied over the centuries by a range of researchers. Stories about final words to deceased loved ones and figures of all kinds, along with descriptions of beautiful landscapes or architecture, appear across decades. Hundreds of stories have been documented and shared about this form of nonreferential communication, and yet, surprisingly, as a culture we are just now beginning to acknowledge and recognize these visions and the words that describe them as a part of the realm that people perceive as they die.

There is a world that the dying seem to enter that is sometimes shared with us briefly. A 2014 research study at the Center for Hospice and Palliative Care demonstrated that end-of-life dreams and visions (ELDVs) are common. Eighty-seven percent of the study's participants reported dreams or visions; 72 percent of those entailed reunions with deceased loved ones, while 52 percent of the visions were related to themes of preparing to go somewhere. The visions appeared months, weeks, days, or hours before death and typically lessened the fear of dying among those experiencing them, making their transition from life to death easier. While it is common for people to experience discomfort, fear, anxiety, and agitation before dying, "a person's fear of death often diminishes as a direct result of ELDVs, and what arises is new insight into mortality.... ELDVs do not deny death, but in fact, [they] transcend the dying experience."

This knowledge is becoming commonly accepted in the medical field, as illustrated by this entry about dying that appears on the mainstream online resource WebMD: "Hallucinations and visions, especially of long-gone loved ones, can be comforting. If seeing and talking to someone who isn't there makes the person who's dying happier, you don't need to try to convince them that they aren't real. It may upset them and make them argue and fight with you."

Health-care professionals tell me that deathbed visions are qualitatively different from hallucinations that result from medications. Hallucinations include images of animals, insects on the walls, dragons, figures such as devils, and visions of people who are critical of the dying but unknown to them. Most hallucinations are described as annoying, sometimes frightening, and easily managed by medication changes. Hallucinations are more likely to be forgotten by the patient, and they occur when the patient is not lucid. Visions, unlike hallucinations or delirium, typically occur in patients who are aware of their environment and are lucid — and these patients often remember their visions clearly. Palliative-care nurse and researcher Madelaine Lawrence explained to me during our interview that when patients have deathbed visions, they are able to "move between worlds lucidly and easily — and this capacity does not exist when a patient is heavily influenced by drug-induced hallucinations."

We saw in the preceding chapter that some dying people who have the ability to move between "worlds" express this with hybrid sentences. For example, a person might say, "Get me a pencil and paper," referring to a real-life pencil and paper, and then say, "I need to write down the names of everyone coming to the big party tonight" — when there is no real party and the listed attendees are all deceased. The person appears to be aware of both the world we know and the one that is unseen to us. Researchers have determined that the dying speak to the figures in their visions in complete sentences, while this does not happen frequently when people have hallucinations. My transcripts and accounts confirm this finding. Many beloveds reported hearing loved ones having complex conversations with deceased friends and relatives.

Martha Jo Atkins, a death educator and counselor, identified the following characteristics associated with the visions of the dying: transcendent experiences, a need to leave, personalized companionship, communication with unseen individuals, positive comfort, and a process of understanding. Both Lawrence and Atkins encourage us to have "positive regard" for the dying person's experience, including whatever visions he or she may have. Lawrence explained to me that it is important that we "validate, validate." The person may be seeing deceased friends or relatives, angels, religious figures, animals, or men in black, or may be hearing beautiful music. It is important to acknowledge the dying person's experience, even though we are not sharing that experience. She also strongly recommends that we support our beloveds by encouraging them to speak freely about what they are seeing. In our interview, she noted, "When someone is dying, they want to be connected emotionally with those who are close to them before they go."

So, while we know that these visions do exist, and that they have qualities that make them significantly different from the hallucinations that result from medications, there is still the question of whether they are merely tricks of a dying brain or actually represent the existence of angels or spirits that help us transition to an afterlife. Could it be that we are somehow biologically programmed to have these comforting visions at a time that otherwise could be terrifying — in the same way that our bodies are flooded with endorphins, or we experience numbing shock, when we have been seriously injured?

My friend and former colleague Dr. Erica Goldblatt Hyatt and I discussed this question one day. "Evolutionary programming is aimed at increasing our survival, right? So why would we be programmed biologically to find comfort or even transcendence in dying?" she asked me. "If we are speaking of pure biological functioning, wouldn't our survival be selected for traits that do not make for a peaceful and comforting death experience?" Her question is a good one. Is it possible that death represents an entirely metaphysical process in which all the rules that might apply to our physical bodies and to survival of the fittest are completely abandoned for something else? Do we leave behind the physical world, and all its rules, including those of literal language, to enter another world that we can perceive only as we look out from the threshold between life and death?

Isabelle Chauffeton Saavedra, a psychic medium, researcher, and author, was raised in a family of scientists and has a firm grounding in physics and mathematics. She has spent her life reconciling the two poles of her life: her scientific training and her psychic work.

One of the many ways she understands her own psychic and mediumistic capabilities is, as she explained to me, through understanding our natural world: "There is a universe we do not see, but this does not mean it does not exist. If you look at the animal kingdom, for example, many animals have access to information that we do not have. Our senses process only a small part of the information that exists in the universe."

Indeed, Isabelle is correct. Consider all the information that other animals perceive that we cannot. Butterflies can see ultraviolet markings on other butterflies, which allows them to find healthier mates. Reindeer rely on ultraviolet light to find food and easily identify a predator's ultraviolet-absorbent urine in ultraviolet-reflective snow. The yellow petals of black-eyed Susans have ultraviolet markings that form a bull's-eye in the center of each blossom, which attracts bees. A number of animals use echolocation to both navigate and hunt. They emit high-frequency sounds, and the "echoes" of these sounds help the animals form images of the landscape. Some species, like electric fish and eels, echolocate with electrical impulses. Using their own voices for echolocation, bats can navigate quickly and accurately. Many animals perceive and respond to the earth's magnetic field. Species ranging from hamsters, salamanders, sparrows, and rainbow trout to spiny lobsters and bacteria engage the magnetic field.

While humans live in a world dominated by sight and sound, pheromones are a primary source of information for many animals. These chemical substances communicate a range of things, from stress and alarm to danger and sexual fertility. Ants have ten to twenty pheromones that they use in structuring their society. The ants actually communicate through the release of these pheromones as if they were constructing words in a sentence.

Communication and information come in many forms throughout the animal kingdom. Human language and senses occupy only one portion of the spectrum of what is perceivable.

Kenneth Ring and Sharon Cooper's research on the blind suggests that human beings potentially have an expanded sense or perception when they are "out of body." We also know that certain changes to our bodies can influence and even expand our perception, as occurs in trance, altered, and enlightened states, mentioned in the preceding chapter.

A fascinating example of how a slight degradation of our senses can lead to expanded perceptions is artist Claude Monet. As the great artist grew older, he developed cataracts. Carl Zimmer writes, "After years of failed treatments, he agreed at age 82 to have the lens of his left eye completely removed." Once his lens had been removed, the blue-tuned pigments in Monet's eyes grabbed "some of the UV light bouncing off of the petals. He started to paint the flowers a whitish-blue." In part, this is what we associate with Monet's unique brilliance — he was able to bring us a view of the world that is often left unobserved.

Isabelle Chauffeton Saavedra explained to me:

When I do remote viewings or psychic readings, I am trying to get all the information embedded in the fabric of the universe. There is so much that we do not perceive with our senses, but does that mean it does not exist?

One example of this was a reading she did for the family of a young man in a coma. As is her customary process, she told the family that she wanted no information in advance from them, because she wanted nothing to keep her from receiving "pure input."

When she meditated, she heard the phrase "Tuesday, Friday, Tuesday, Friday" in the voice of a man. It made no sense to her at the moment, but she found out later that those were the days he was visited by his family. "This kind of thing happens all the time," she explained. Without context, those words made little sense, which is much like the way Malynda Cress described the unintelligibility of "Tell me about the birds." Isabelle said, "The information that seems nonsensical is most likely the most powerful piece of information, because it is the information not filtered or understood by my analytic mind." She told me that when she does a reading, she is trying to get information from the realm of the unseen. "Everything in the unseen is information embedded in the fabric of the universe. The role of the psychic is to tap that."

Isabelle and other psychics I interviewed explained that information from and about those who have died lies in that vast field not perceived by the five-sense, three-dimensional brain, the brain that processes language. Isabelle paraphrased Antoine-Laurent Lavoisier, an eighteenth-century French chemist: "Nothing's created, nothing's lost, everything changes to another form." She told me, "What he said was meant to be applied to chemistry at the time, but it is actually the fundamental principle of our universe. Your loved ones were here at the beginning of everything, as you were — and they still are."

We know that we perceive only a limited field of information, given our five senses. Isabelle suggested, "There are things that make sense to the dying, not to others, halfway between material and immaterial. They have a glimpse of the whole world of the unseen."

Did we come from this vast universe of the unseen? Do we return to it? Can our language track the pathway from this three-dimensional world to that other one? Perhaps the nonreferential language of the dying is an indication that it can.

CHAPTER EIGHT

Lullabies and Good-Byes

Is Our First and Final Language Unspoken?

There was no speaking, as the person's lips never moved,
and neither did mine. But there were words.
It was a question: "Are you ready?"
— *Tim, Final Words Project participant*

While other species communicate in a number of ways, ranging from pheromones to echolocation, no others have the physical and cognitive apparatus to produce the complex spoken language of *Homo sapiens*.

The iconic phrase "In the beginning was the Word" resonates strongly when we look at the importance of language in the creation of human life and culture. Our ability to speak and develop complex language distinguishes us from other members of the animal kingdom. It is as if words literally breathe us into existence and give us the tools to create the important social connections that have made it possible for humans to survive. Larger animals could have wiped out our ancestors, but language was among a handful of attributes that helped us thrive.

When a child is born, he or she can perceive 800 or so different sounds, called phonemes, which can be combined to form the words of languages around the world. When a child reaches about six months of age, a mysterious portal opens in the infant's brain.

Suddenly the baby is ready to begin learning the native language. Of the 800 potential phonemes, the infant will master only those specific to his or her native language. This might mean as few as 11 phonemes if the child learns Rotokas, a language of Papua New Guinea, or as many as 112 phonemes if the child learns !Xóõ, a language of Botswana — or some number in between if the child learns, for example, English, with 44 phonemes. This period of acquiring phonemes is what neuroscientists call the "sensitive period" and lasts only a few months, but it is extended in children exposed to sounds of a second language.

While the infant's babbling is nonsense, linguists know that these sounds are also the foundation of language acquisition. Within a matter of two to three years, most humans learn to recognize the sounds of, and acquire the basic structures of, their language, which allows them to speak with their caregivers and peers.

By seven years of age, most of us lose the plasticity that allows us to learn other languages with the ease and fluency of earlier years. As our words take shape, our world takes shape; and literal language, grounded in this three-dimensional, five-sense reality, is carved out of what begins as a vast potential that we hear as babbling.

Telepathy May Be Our First Form of Communication

So, how is it that *Homo sapiens* has survived, given that our primary means of communication — spoken language — is not well formed at infancy, the most vulnerable time of our lives? Although it takes months, even years, for humans to speak a native language, our caregivers often understand what we need — and our survival is assured.

Many would say that this happens because babies "speak" to parents through cries and screams. This is true, but often parents seem to "just know" what their cooing and crying babies want and need. Many parents have described that while they may not be able to understand the cries of another parent's child, they seem to sense or feel what their own offspring need.

Researchers Geoffrey Leigh, Jean Metzker, and Nathan Metzker explain that this may be a result of a unique way that parents and their young children communicate. The research team investigated language in communications between parent and infant at the beginning of the language acquisition continuum, discussed in their unpublished 2012 paper "Essence Theory." Their studies indicate that parents and infants communicate energetically and "telepathically" before spoken language is fully mastered. As infants gain spoken language, the ability to communicate in nonverbal ways diminishes. They explain that the same kind of communication that is documented in near-death experiences as "telepathic and nonlinguistic" can occur in the communications between babies and their caregivers.

This form of communication bypasses the physical apparatus of the voice box and the articulation of a native language's phonemes and strings of words and ideas. Could the nonlinguistic communication described by near-death experiencers also exist between parents and infants and represent a form of communication on both sides of the threshold? As you may recall, telepathic communication is one of the important hallmarks in the descriptions of those who have died and come back again. The following two descriptions are from people I interviewed for the Final Words Project:

> My mother, who died several years ago, spoke to me. I understood everything. I was supposed to follow her. There were no real words, not the way we think of words. I just knew to go with her — her whole being communicated with me.

This figure, this figure of light, was speaking to me through thoughts. We were talking, communicating in the most profound way without one word spoken — or what we think of as words. He just knew everything I thought and everything about me.

The articulation of words through the voice box corresponds to our manifestation in this world. As we move away from the world, so does our reliance on spoken language to form connections to our external environment.

Final Words Project participant Sue Ronnenkamp shared these stories of communicating in new nonverbal ways with her dying mother:

> Mom was a great connector, in fact one of the best. But then, after her stroke, everything changed. I clearly remember sitting all afternoon in silence with Mom in her room one day. I sat and read in her rocking chair, and she was in her recliner dozing or simply being silent. Before dinner, a nurse's aide came into the room for her predinner check. Mom perked up at that point and introduced me to the aide and then said, "My daughter and I have been having a wonderful conversation." She was so sincere with her words that I was forced to shift my perspective. Maybe somehow we were communicating like we used to do, but on a level I didn't have access to that afternoon. Following that incident, I gave in and surrendered to the silence and eased into *being* with Mom in a whole new way.
>
> Over time, I learned to listen very closely when she did speak and share things with me. What I discovered was that my old mom was still inside her. Her wisdom and insights took my breath away at times.... She knew things in ways

I still don't understand. For example, she knew when I became involved with a new boyfriend even though nothing had been shared about this with anyone in my family. This made me realize that a mother's sixth sense may be stronger than we even realize.

Leigh, Metzker, and Metzker suggest, "It may be our infants who teach us about 'reality' in the sense of a larger energetic and conscious connection even when we see the bodies as separate." In the authors' discussion, they propose the notion of essence — and that essence exists beyond as well as before verbal language acquisition.

The telepathic bonds that exist between loved ones, especially parents and children, become very clear in our dying days, as we saw in the example of Sue, above. The Reverend Cari Rush Willis shared a story of the powerful bond between a mother and her dying daughter, who were separated by continents (I also received several other examples of stories illustrating this kind of communication across distances):

Before my dear friend Yukiko died, her friend and I were sitting by her bedside listening to the silence and taking in the beauty of our beloved friend. She then turned to us and very quietly said, "My mom was here. We had the best conversation. It was so good to see her again." Yukiko went on to tell us the small details of the conversation.

Yukiko's friend whispered to me: "Her mom lives in Japan. There is no way she was here."

I asked Yukiko, "Do you remember the time that she was here?"

She replied, "Oh, yes!" right away, with as much enthusiasm as her small and frail body could muster as she told us the exact time.

The next day as I was sitting beside Yukiko, her long-time friend entered the room with an excited look on her face. I could tell she was about ready to burst with the news she was about to tell me, so I remained silent.

"You know that story about Yukiko's mother yesterday."

"Yes, of course."

"Well, I emailed Yukiko's mother, as I normally do in order to give her a status update on Yukiko. You won't believe this, but Yukiko's mom said that she was talking to Yukiko at the same exact time, about the same exact things! Isn't that unreal!"

I smiled at her. And I said, "A mother's love is outside time and space — how wonderful that we have proof of that!

Terri Daniel, author of *Embracing Death* and *A Swan in Heaven*, describes the remarkable evolution of her telepathic/psychic gifts as her terminally ill son, Daniel, lost his ability to speak:

As my telepathic skills were increasing, Danny's ability to speak was diminishing. Before the onset of his illness, he was a normal boy with superior language skills, but as the disease progressed, he gradually lost the power of speech along with most of his other physical abilities. During the latter part of his illness he could express himself well enough to let me know if he was hungry or cold, and respond to simple questions with one-word answers. But by the time he died, he had been completely without words for nearly two years. We had learned to communicate using a natural form of telepathy similar to the way mothers communicate with their pre-verbal children.

Could it be, then, that as we die, the language that articulates our personal and cultural identities throughout life gives way to the language of what Leigh, Metzker, and Metzker call "essence"? That is, we return to what might be considered our essential way of communicating as we leave the physical plane where our personalities developed. Is it possible that as we pass the threshold, some of us return to what seems like babbling, as if we are crossing through the very portal of language from which life begins?

Shape-Shifting: Symbols and Early Speech

Nurse Susan Lynch explained in a Facebook post, "I have been a labor nurse for twenty-four years and have been with many people passing over. I always knew I would finish my career in hospice or palliative care, some form of end-of-life nursing. Many think this is strange, but truly they are one and the same."

Winn Mallard, the daughter of a minister, was so moved by what she witnessed in her father's final days that she wrote the book *Death Is a Miracle*. Winn transcribed and shared her father's final words with me over a period of several months. One day she sent me an email about a conversation she had had with Mary, a veteran hospice social worker, in which they discussed the similarities between infants and the dying. Winn talked about how similar were the transitions of birth and death:

> Just as every woman and newborn have their unique way of labor and entrance, so does each human have their own unique way of leaving this realm. Sometimes quick and easy, sometimes slow and easy, sometimes intense labor, sometimes not. Babies get the hiccups a lot...so does daddy-o. Babies need to be fed, so does daddy-o. And once toddlers begin getting words, they often talk nonsense, messages that come from a place beyond the senses.

The connection between nonsense in our first days and its emergence in our final days is compelling. Similarly, the prevalence of references to basic shapes such as circles and boxes in the transcripts of the dying is also compelling. Those who research early childhood development have established that humans have an inborn ability to understand shapes. Babies can recognize the difference between a circle and a square. Shapes are one of the most basic ways that humans map the world around them. Like the phonemes that form the template on which our spoken language is based, shapes form the blueprint that allows us to develop spatial awareness and understanding; they also serve as the foundation for reading and writing. Is it possible that as we die, we return to some of the most essential cognitive elements as our connection to this world deconstructs? Could it be that these primary visual elements are connected to the unseen world?

William Stillman would argue that this could be the case. Stillman is a highly regarded psychic medium and author of twelve books about autism. He himself has Asperger's syndrome and has researched the unique symbolic iconography of both autistics and psychics. He talks about how those with autism have trouble verbalizing the rich symbolic world in which they live. His books overflow with examples of people who are autistic and live in a world of symbols that bypass the verbal channel of speech. He has demonstrated in various cases that this silent world is rich in precognitive awareness and telepathic connections. Many of those he researched heard thoughts or voices much like those described by people who have had near-death experiences.

Stillman explained to me during our interviews that he, like Isabelle, often gets his most accurate information in both symbolic and nonsensical form. He has discovered that the "nonsensical" symbols that emerge during his psychic readings actually have their own consistent meanings and organization. Stillman calls this collection of symbols a "lexicon of spiritual iconography." The symbols are consistent — that is, they represent certain meanings that he has come to understand and remember. When he is doing a psychic reading and sees an image of swollen ankles, for example, that always means the person receiving the reading has a family history of diabetes. However, these symbols became intelligible to him only after repeated occurrences over time.

He explained to me that "spiritual iconography is like an ethereal version of charades for advanced players." A gas stove with a burner left on represents Alzheimer's or some other form of dementia. When he sees roses, this is a spiritual communication acknowledging a celebration. A vision of the laying down of arms (in the form of someone placing a firearm in the client's lap) symbolizes a father figure making an apology. "It took me eleven years to become relatively fluent in my personal spiritual iconography," Stillman said. "No two people have the same icons when they are receiving psychic information. The icons are based on our personal experiences and how our mind represents things symbolically."

His research demonstrates that a large percentage of the autistic subjects he studied also had deeply embedded iconographies. Often those who live in a highly symbolic world are challenged by the need to articulate and organize what they know and see into spoken language. He believes, as I do, that the realm of the unseen is a world of symbols and metaphors — just as we often see in the language of the dying.

Stillman also suggested that the nonsense we hear in the spoken words of the autistic may be a kind of "by-product," like exhaust from a car, but in this case a by-product of leaving behind the traditional ways of processing language to engage in a more symbolic, unspoken one. This seems to parallel some of Newberg's research into the regions of the brain that are associated with mystical states and with a decrease in purposeful, meaningful language. The nonsense of autism and the nonsense associated with dying may both reflect a shift away from the functioning or processing of the more purposeful, literally oriented language centers.

In infancy, those language centers are not yet developed and are on their way to gaining the sound-making and cognitive structures that allow for meaningful and purposeful language. Perhaps as the dying reach the threshold, and as the young hear the portal door close behind them, they share a common understanding. Both the dying and the young may have access to another way of communication and perceiving.

One man described how his father in his final days seemed particularly attuned to his young grandson as he watched the toddler playing. "How can that baby be in both worlds at once?" the dying man asked. Unfortunately, those who were present did not ask the father what he was seeing or exactly what he meant.

Jerry told me, during our interview, about a moment that had taken place during his grandmother's dying days, and which had stuck with him for years. One of his nieces was only two years old at the time, and she had sat on the bed with the grandmother. "They were face-to-face, eye-to-eye, and both spoke babbling nonsense. I remember watching in awe as they spoke with these waves of sounds — and they both seemed to understand. They were having this very private conversation. It was like they totally got each other," he said laughing. As language took hold in the toddler, it loosened in the lips of the senior.

Cheryl Espinosa-Jones related that when her partner, Joanne, died at age forty-five, their young daughter was highly attuned to her passing:

The night before, as Joanne was leaving her body, and she was so close to death, our daughter wailed out with such intensity that it brought Joanne back into her body for one more night. The next day, however, our daughter ran into the room without any fear. My wife died peacefully, quite beautifully. Soon after Joanne's passing, my daughter pointed to the bedroom ceiling and said, "Mommy, look! Look at all the birds!" That seemed very significant to all of us in the room, as if beings were coming to help her wherever it is we go. She had entered the realm of the unseen with Joanne, who she called JiJo.

The next night, my daughter slept with me; and then in the middle of the night, there was a big thud as she fell onto the floor. This woke me up with a start and was very unusual for her.

I asked her what had happened. She told me, "I saw JiJo on a ladder going up — and she was on the top...and I wanted to go with her, but she said, 'No, no, honey you have to go back down!'" With those words, the young girl fell to the floor.

The themes in this story are ones I saw in other transcripts too: birds and ladders emerge in descriptions of the unseen, as do admonitions that only the dead or dying can enter certain territory, where the living must not go. The clarity of the child's vision is startling and makes me wonder what worlds we do not see as we move through our ordinary lives, only to return to them, perhaps, in our final days.

The following account submitted to the final Words Project website shares the words of a child who had unexpected knowledge. A woman whose mother had just died received a call from her brother, Bret: "He said that his eight-year-old daughter, Sarah, woke up that morning and said, 'I know that Grammy is an angel now. And she's young again.' No one had told her yet that Grammy had died."

The Interior Language of a Coma

Our spoken language often fades away at the end of life, but nurse and researcher Madelaine Lawrence indicates that consciousness does not. Her research on coma survivors offers some compelling insights into states of unconsciousness.

Lawrence determined through her interviews with 111 people who had survived comas that 27 percent heard, understood, and responded emotionally at some point to what was said while they were presumed to be unconscious. Another 23 percent of those interviewed had experienced extrasensory perception, including near-death experiences and out-of-body experiences. Her research in hospital units and in the literature reveals that more than 70 percent of individuals who regain consciousness after a coma remember events that took place during their unconscious period.

This comment from Robert, one of the people Lawrence interviewed, demonstrates that comatose people are often much more aware than others think: "If anyone asked me, I would swear that I never passed out. As far as I'm concerned I went through the whole thing awake." However, his nurse described him differently: "His eyes rolled back in his head and he went out."

Harvey, another of those interviewed by Lawrence, explained:

It was very strange. All I could imagine was that maybe I was dead. I didn't know what it's like to be dead, but I thought I could hear but nothing more. No sensation, and I couldn't see. The only thing I recall when I heard him [the doctor] say, "We are losing him," was trying to say something like, "I'm okay...I'm not dead or anything." I think I tried to talk to them, but I couldn't. It was like I had no muscular coordination. I was thinking the words but not saying them....Then I think I began to be able to speak, and I did say a few things to them...the first thing I regained was my voice.

Lawrence explains, "Hearing is not the last to go, consciousness is." The interviewees reported having internal dialogue even when they could not hear external information. They had experienced a continued sense of self no matter what their connections were to the external world. Our ability to communicate within ourselves and think about that communication can still function when our external awareness is no longer operating. This inner sense of "me" remains intact long after the other functions of the brain shut down.

This continuity of self was expressed in coma survivors' awareness of and sensitivity to the emotional energy of the people around them. Carol, another of Lawrence's research participants, reported that although she was in a coma, she could recognize her children, husband, doctors, ministers, nurses, and even the housekeeping personnel who came close to the bed. She explained, "I also knew there was a love affair or a thing going on between one of the nurses and one of the doctors. It was like I could read their minds."

Patients were aware of their own emotions as well. In one instance, Carol overheard a doctor say that there was "nothing on the left side," and that she would probably be a "vegetable." This made her angry. One of the patients told a nurse that he had tried so hard to tell his brother that he was all right and wasn't the vegetable the doctor had said he was, but that he hadn't been able to communicate. In another instance, a patient called a nursing unit after she had been discharged to leave a message for a nurse. She said, "Tell the nurse who said I was going to be a vegetable, that I'm not."

Lawrence writes, "When the physical body system is compromised through severe physiological conditions...the conscious mind is replaced by another system that permits extrasensory experiences to happen....During extrasensory experiences, the subjects typically reported receiving information telepathically." The study seems to indicate that even when the mechanisms that connect us with our world are disabled, something within us continues. This "me" that endures appears to be particularly sensitive to the energy and emotions of others and can and does understand telepathically. These findings corroborate the work of Leigh, Metzker, and Metzker in which they suggest that there is an essential self who communicates in our early years in ways that are nonverbal. The findings are also consistent with the work of Kenneth Ring and Sharon Cooper, in which blind NDE survivors explained having been able to "see" through a kind of transcendental awareness, even though they were clinically dead at the time. No matter what happens physiologically, the internal communication mechanism can function while the external one does not.

The Sunset Day: Food and Forgiveness

The inner voice seems to emerge with resounding clarity in the window of time before death that many health-care providers call the *sunset day* and researchers call *terminal lucidity*. Hospice workers told me that the sunset day usually occurs a few days before the person dies and offers at least a few minutes, and sometimes a whole day, in which the dying person suddenly has heightened lucidity, a livelier appearance, and more energy. The term *terminal lucidity*, which refers to the same phenomenon, was coined several years ago by German biologist Michael Nahm in his 2009 article in the *Journal of Near-Death Studies*.

People I interviewed described how their loved ones who had been relatively nonresponsive suddenly emerged from their deeply internal and quiet state and spoke words of kindness, reassurance, or guidance for a short time before dying. Several people described a kind of glow or lightness around their beloved. This email summarizes what I heard often: "In those days before he died, he grew luminous. His face cleared and his eyes widened."

The term *sunset day* is often used because the burst of lucidity shortly before death reminds people of the sun's bright rays that flood the sky as it sets into the horizon. In my interviews with people, two themes emerged in our discussions of the sunset day: final pleasures and final reconciliations.

Rick's father, Dave, was eighty-one and dying of cancer. In those last days he spent most of his time sleeping in his bedroom on the second floor of his old house, only steps away from his favorite sitting spot — a balcony overlooking a small lake. Throughout his life, he had savored summer evenings with a cold beer in his hand. Four days before dying, he stirred from sleep, sat up, and said to his sons: "Take me out to the balcony. I want to get a look at the lake. Get me a beer, too, would you? A nice cold one." His family lovingly carried him out so he could sit in his favorite chair as he enjoyed one last bottle of beer.

Cynthia shared this story about her father's sunset day:

One of the clearest indications that my father was dying was that he could not eat. For most of his life, eating was a celebrated ritual. In the days and weeks before dying, he did not want to eat or drink anything. Until three days before he died, my daughter and I were home alone with him. The man who seemed frozen in silence emerged from his sleep and said, "I feel like having some pot roast — the pot roast you cook. And I would love some pineapple upside-down cake. I would love that."

My daughter and I were stunned. We cooked for him all morning, and then served him the way he used to love it. He sat up with strength — he had not sat up for weeks — and bit into the pot roast like old times. Then he started talking about his granddaughter and how I better take good care of her...get her guitar lessons...and how he was worried about his daughter-in-law and her health. We had him again for five hours...and then, just as suddenly as he came back to life he seemed to return to dying...and he was gone in a few days.

Another Final Words Project participant told me, "My dad was one of those who did not eat for the week preceding his death; and then before he actually passed, he woke up ravenous and ate huge meals at breakfast and then again at lunch right before he passed that evening."

Tara described the final words of her father-in-law, Sam:

All the years I was married, my husband's dad teased me a lot about my weight and my appearance. It was all supposed to be in good fun, but I never found it funny. Matter of fact, it just hurt. Before he died, he was sleeping a lot, but then one day, just a few days before he died, he seemed alert. I went into his room, and he told me to come close to him. He looked at me and said in the most tender voice I ever heard from him: "I never noticed how pretty you are. I am so sorry I never noticed."

Christine Zagelow shared this story of her mother's sunset day:

I walked into the hospital room, and my mom said, "God came to me at four o'clock this morning." She looked better than she had looked in weeks. She was sitting up in bed, her eyes alert, and her articulation very clear. I asked her what had happened, but it was difficult for her to explain, other than to say that God appeared to her and was still at the end of her bed touching her right foot. I wondered if she could have been healed. She was so alert compared to previous days and speaking with much energy. She then said, "Oh, look at that beautiful card, and what a beautiful thing to say! And oh, that one, what wonderful friends and family I have." She was reading each one carefully from her bed after I placed them on the wall. The wall was approximately fifteen to twenty feet from her bed. My mother had worn corrective lenses since the fifth grade, and I had never known her to see from that distance before without her glasses. Had her eyesight improved as well as her health? I was amazed by her appearance. Had God cured her of cancer? Had a miracle occurred?

Soon after, her mother passed away.

Several people I interviewed shared stories of sitting at the bedside of a loved one who was nonresponsive and noncommunicative, and who, right before dying, sat up and seemed fully aware of who was in the room and what was going on. One middle-aged man I interviewed, Jason, described how his brother, who had been in a deep sleep for days, stirred and his torso rose. "He looked right at me. At first it frightened me, but then I felt this deep connection. My brother said, 'I am all right.'" And then Jason's brother proceeded to lie back down; two days later, he was gone.

Similar accounts include the following:

> "My mother was in a coma for three weeks. One day, her eyes popped open. She looked at me and said, 'Tell everyone I am okay and that I love them.' She died five hours later."

> "My mother had not communicated in days. I was thinking I needed a break from all this. Then my mother began to move. I prayed, got a chair, and

an hour later her upper body rose. She looked right at me and said, 'I love you.'"

"Bill had not spoken in weeks. I sat next to him, waiting, hoping he would say something. And then, one evening, he opened his eyes, reached out his hand, and said, 'It's not what you think,' and then sank back into wordlessness and died two days later."

Hospice nurse Beverly Garcia, after hearing stories of her patients' short bursts of lucidity before dying, experienced something similar with her own mother. Beverly's mother was a very reserved woman. "My mother could never tell me that she loved me; but then close to a day before she died, she broke a long spell of silence and told me, 'I love you, Beverly, I always have.'"

Jeffrey K. told the following story about his mother:

She had been fading quickly for about seven days...not eating, unable to manage the stairs. The last couple of days she became kind of snoozy, drifting in and out. The last day she was basically comatose. In the evening, I started to go out just to take a break; but when I told my father I planned to do this, she stirred and groaned, and I decided to stay put. About two hours later, as I was sitting in a chair beside her bed, she came back into consciousness and lifted the upper part of her torso up. I put my arms around her, and she looked into my eyes searchingly. Then, she said twice: "Help me, help me." I said, "I've done everything I can.... Now you're at the edge. Go for the light." Then she collapsed back, so I laid her back down flat and watched her breathing slow down and stop, within perhaps three minutes.

Jordan White explained how he was stunned by his mother's coherence a few days before she died, when she started talking about the files in the study that held all the family financial information. Her Alzheimer's disease had led to nerve cell death and tissue loss; with time, her brain had shrunk dramatically, affecting nearly all its functions. Knowing this, he wondered whether his mother's debilitated brain was truly responsible for the production of language and awareness in those final words. Who or what was it that lovingly told her son of the location of the files after not having spoken lucidly in years?

Of all those I interviewed about the sunset day, no one had a story in which angry or spiteful words were spoken during that window of lucidity. Most of the stories included final requests for favorite foods or final reconciliations or pronouncements of love, even from those who had never expressed those words in the course of their lives. It's possible to imagine that at a time of clear thinking, a dying parent could just as easily have said to his son, "For goodness' sake, isn't it time you got a decent job and dumped that wife of yours? Here I am on my deathbed, and you have not dignified my life in any way!"

Bruce Greyson, professor of psychiatry and neurobehavioral sciences at the University of Virginia, and Michael Nahm in Freiburg, Germany, have begun to take a careful look at the sunset-day phenomenon. Professor Alexander Batthyany, who teaches cognitive science at the University of Vienna, is currently running a large-scale study on terminal lucidity, the first of its kind.

Almost all brain scientists have assumed up until now that a severely damaged brain makes normal cognition impossible. But Batthyany suggests that normal cognition, or lucidity, does occur in spite of a severely damaged brain, as in the cases mentioned above. He notes that it happens in about 5 to 10 percent of Alzheimer's cases, and only when death is very near.

Terminal lucidity has been known to occur even when the patient's speech center has been destroyed, and some dying individuals have gained mobility where they previously had none. It's a remarkable area of medicine, one that has been only minimally studied, even though plentiful anecdotes have been collected over time. These accounts may suggest a crucial distinction between the brain, which obviously dies, and the self — the user of the brain — which might not.

Unspoken Connections: Reaching

Death educator Martha Jo Atkins reported to me that, "as people come very close to death, they often speak less and start reaching, as if to something or someone. One hand goes up, and then it moves in a symphony of motion. A change often sweeps across the person's face — sometimes the person's upper body brightens."

I remember that for a moment, in the last days of my father's life, his hands were pointed toward the ceiling and were fluttering like butterflies. His hands reached up and his fingers stroked the air; it was as if he were reaching to someone I could not see.

The following comment from Rachel was typical among Final Words Project participants: "When my mom was in her final hour of life, she was asleep, and then suddenly she woke up, looked into the corner of the room, and put her hands out like she was reaching out for somebody." Often in the last days, few words are spoken, but the essence of the person still very much remains.

Melinda Ziemer, a therapist, writes in her article "End-of-Life Care: The Spirituality of Living When Dying":

I know from experience that if you're not afraid to look into the eyes of the dying, you'll often find that their eyes wordlessly reveal the secret beauty of the innermost self. For me, the dying gave a new meaning to the expression "the eyes of the heart." One desires to respond to that gaze with a look that says, "I understand that all the fullness of your life is in this moment and that it is an honour to be able to look into your eyes. The approach of death doesn't frighten me. I want to be here with you. This moment is yours."

In the following story, Winn Mallard talks about her connection with her father despite the changes and reduction in his ability to speak:

Daddy-o was so excited to see me yesterday, and after joyful greetings he asked, "And who are you?" His body slightly flinched when I said, "I'm Winn." Then he asked, "How do I know you as Winn?" And after a few minutes of pondering, I said, "Well, what does your heart tell you? Do you feel a familiar flicker in your heart? Does it feel comfortable to be in my presence?" He gazed deeply into my eyes for many moments. I said, "In your heart do you feel me? In your heart are we one?" while we stared deeply into each other via our crystal windows. He repeated my questions as statements; perhaps he felt it. I sure did! Daddy-o and I are one, and we have eternity.

Life begins wordlessly and, in many cases, ends the same way. Where we come from and where we go may, indeed, be the same place, and we may use the same nonlinguistic language — an unspoken one shared between hearts and minds — in both places. This kind of nonverbal communication was identified in the dreams and visions of the dying by Pei C. Grant, director of research at the Palliative Care Institute, who has done extensive research. She writes, "A statement we heard from people is that very little is said in their dreams and visions, but they extract huge meaning and comfort from them."

Hospice nurse Judy Warren had a number of telepathic connections with her patients over thirty years. She would communicate in what she calls the "language of the soul." She explained that, as she stood at her patients' bedsides, she could see, hear, and feel information that later she discovered to be true. This ranged from final requests to specific information about when they would die. She described how the doctors she worked with came to rely on her mysterious ability to know when a patient would die. "The doctors, of course, did not know that I was telepathically communicating with patients, but they knew I was often right."

Malynda Cress, a hospice volunteer, reports having many experiences in which she hears, sees, and feels her dying patients' inner thoughts and feelings — including information about when they will die. She has learned of details that she otherwise could not have known about her patients' lives, as well as what patients wanted from or wished to share with family members and friends before dying.

How does this "language of the soul" differ from literal and ordinary language? Psychics and near-death experiencers explain that communication in the world of the unseen does not need physical structures, such as vocal cords. While the sounds associated with spoken language are sequenced in time, telepathic communications are not. Communication is nonlinguistic and sometimes simultaneous. Raymond Moody shared a quote with me that came from his friend and mentor Dr. George Ritchie. Ritchie had had a near-death experience and described communication in this way: "Hypocrisy is not possible in the afterlife. What you say is the same as what you think." Ritchie explained that thought and communication during an NDE are one; they occur simultaneously. It is impossible, therefore, to think one thing and say another as we often do in our ordinary five-sense, three-dimensional lives.

CHAPTER NINE

I'll Call You When I Get There

After-Death Communication

Do not cry too long,
let that laughter of your love
illuminate the skies,
for I will always hear you
— *Automatic writing inspired by my father*

As we saw earlier, it is possible that communication begins in childhood telepathically, and that we return to this nonlinguistic "language of the soul" when we die. The stories of after-death communication offer a chance for us to consider that both communication and consciousness continue beyond the threshold via the symbolic and telepathic means discussed in the previous chapter.

When I first set out to do final-words research, I had no intention of writing about or researching afterlife communication; however, people of all walks of life shared their stories of compelling synchronicities. It became clear to me that any discussion of words at the threshold would be incomplete without at least a brief look at these accounts. The ones I've included here reflect only a small portion of the stories shared with me. In fact, many more people experienced some kind of communication after death than I had ever imagined.

Bill and Judy Guggenheim's After-Death Communication Project, which was founded in 1988, reported having received thousands of accounts of after-death communication. Julia Assante, in her book *The Last Frontier*, writes, "The percentage of people re-porting contact with the dead in surveys ranges anywhere from 42 to 72 percent. Widows having contact with their deceased hus-bands can go as high as 92 percent. If the surveys had included children and deathbed encounters, which are extremely common, the percentages would have been even heftier. A whopping 75 per-cent of parents who lost a child had an encounter within a year of the child's death. But a sad 75 percent of all those who had encounters reported not mentioning them to anyone for fear of ridicule."

We saw in the previous chapter, for example, that while hos-pice nurse Judy Warren was accurate enough for doctors to rely on her prognoses for her dying patients, she did not tell the phy-sicians that her knowledge of when patients were going to die had anything to do with telepathic messages from those patients. This certainly would have reduced the credibility she had cultivated over her three-decade nursing career.

However, many people — from psychiatrists to teachers to plumbers to accountants — shared accounts with me of their com-munications with the dying and the dead. The following is based on information from an assistant professor of pharmaceutical and biomedical sciences, whose "telepathic" encounters changed his thinking about the survival of consciousness.

When he was an undergraduate student in chemistry, he was naturally a skeptic and expected things to be proven to him with facts. However, his thinking changed during the time he worked in a morgue. The young academic described how, when he was working with the dead, he had the distinct feeling that people were standing in the room looking at him. It was as if the unseen were speaking with him telepathically, and the message was always the same. "The spirits of the dead were checking in on their bodies to make sure everything was okay," he told me. It was then that he came to believe that consciousness survives: "Everything else in nature and life gets recycled. Why not consciousness?"

After working at the mortuary, the young man got a job delivering pizzas. One night he was sent to a nondescript building with no signs. When he walked in, he was struck with the feeling that many people had died there — but they were "generic or blank people." There were no faces or other specific details in the images he saw in this mind. He had the sense that they were like babies or almost babies.

"Is this an abortion clinic?" he asked someone working there. Yes, the person replied, it was.

He received information in nonverbal ways. In the case of the abortion clinic, the information came to him as both images and the feelings of the faceless. While the scientist's account is remarkable, especially since it comes from a born skeptic, it is by no means unique.

Participants shared with me a wide range of communications from the dying and the dead. Among these are accounts of people's premonitions of dying. In my interviews, I heard several stories demonstrating that people who will soon die often seem to have precognitive awareness of their impending deaths.

Premonitions of Death

Sarah Brightwood, whose seventeen-year-old daughter died tragically in a car accident, found a beautiful poem left behind on her teenager's desk. Her daughter wrote it on February 4, 2015, three days before she died. It was penned the day she left to spend two days with her boyfriend. The car accident occurred as she was driving back home. In Sarah's experience, these were Emily's last words:

Where I Belong

I am hardly overwhelmed
By the dark of the Morning
Or the glow of the Night.
Whether it is the Sun or the Moon
Whispering their sweet rhapsody
Into the majestic heavens
I find infinite quiet
In each wild moment
Knowing that I have a place
Here below the gleaming stars
And undulating clouds.
With my feet in the earth
And my arms outstretched
Embracing the Sky —
I belong.

Sarah wrote me in an email, "There was another amazing thing that Emily left behind. I didn't notice until a few days after Emily's death that she had assembled these words on the fridge":

come
spend
infinite time
away

Her daughter's final words, indeed, seemed to express a gentle and wise awareness of the events that were to unfold in the days ahead.

My father, too, seemed to have a premonition of his death. He appeared in hundreds of photos over the decades, but one stands out as the most memorable. Six weeks before he died, and before there was any indication that death was near, he was vacationing with my mother in Mexico. A friend had joined them, and on one sunny day, with camera in hand, she turned to my father and said, "Morty, here's a pen, write something on your palm that reveals a little about you." In big black letters he wrote "visitor," and then he laughed and said, "I am just visiting the planet!"

Dreams Warning Us of Death

Dreams often let us know when the death of someone we love is approaching, and they can also warn us of our own risk of dying. The following account shares a dream that does both.

Tom dreamed that the atmospheric dome around the earth collapsed, and he reached up his arms to prevent its fall and keep all those on earth from suffocating. That night a good friend of his, Florence, entered the hospital for the last time, gasping for breath as she died. At the time, he attributed the dream to her death that evening. Later in the year, Tom began having trouble with his own respiratory system. He recalled his dream of the collapsing dome and its precognitive quality in relation to Florence. He felt the image was also a warning to him. After convincing doctors to take his concerns seriously, they discovered that one of his arteries was completely blocked and deformed. "I know that the only reason that I am alive to share this tale," he told friends in a Facebook post, "is because I recognized the importance of the dream."

He Said Good-Bye in My Dream

Dreams offer us not only insight but also a forum for those we love who are dying, or have recently died, to communicate with us. Sophia Diamond shared this story about her father, one that is typical of others I heard:

He came to me in a dream and said, "I gotta go now, gotta go. I have no choice. I gotta go." I saw him drift by me, like he was leaving somewhere. A few days after I awoke from this vision dream, my father passed away. I did tell him prior to his dying: "If you die and leave me, may you send me a rainbow and let me know if there is 'another side.'" And, yes, after his funeral, I had a huge rainbow in my backyard.

Rainbows appear in the accounts of several people I spoke with — during, before, or after death. The rationalist's explanation, of course, is that these things occur naturally and then we ascribe meaning to them, especially out of our pain and grief. This may be true in some cases, but there are so many of these stories that simple coincidence does not seem to explain them all. Synchronicities abound in life, especially in the days and weeks right after someone dies.

Christine Zagelow had this synchronistic dream about her brother, Mick, the night after his death:

> Mick came to me in a dream. He was in brown leather motorcycle gear and standing next to the movie actor James Dean, who also rode motorcycles. The next morning, two of Mick's motorcycle buddies came into the house and wanted to know if Mick came to me in a dream. They gave each other the high five, because Mick had told them he would come to me in a dream to show them he made it [to the "other side"], and that he would find James Dean when he got there.

The Beloved Is Beaming and Healthy

Terri Segal, a marriage and family therapist, shared this dream with me about her brother, which she also published in the *Journal for Spiritual and Consciousness Studies* in 2015:

After Duffy's passing, I started experiencing extraordinary things. The first, just two days after he passed, was a dream visitation in which Duffy appeared beaming and healthy and a bit younger. He called me by his nickname for me, T. In a small room I walked towards him, acknowledging how happy I was to see him. He smiled big and called out "Hey T!" As I got closer, he faded out slowly. I asked him to stay but he kept disappearing and then I woke up. There was a vividness to his voice, a clarity to his presence. He directly spoke to me. After that, many synchronicities started to happen.

It's Not Time to Check Out

My mother shared this dream about my father six weeks after he died. She believes it was a message from him, reassuring her that she still had time before dying. "Your dad and I were traveling, as we often did. He went into the hotel, but I could not get into the room. And then I realized I was supposed to check out of the hotel, but I did not have the key. I then heard your father say, 'You have plenty of time before checking out, but when your time comes, I have the key.'"

Although she had never before believed in after-death communication, she felt a strong connection to him and profound reassurance. She laughed and said, "The message was clear: It's not checkout time yet for me!"

These "visitation" dreams from loved ones often have qualities very different from those of our regular dreams. The distinguishing qualities include colors that are much brighter, deeper, and richer than in waking dreams. People report the same thing about the quality of colors during a near-death experience. Often, the beloved is not only seen in the dream but is also, in some way, deeply felt — people even describe feeling touched in some way. Sometimes, there is synesthesia in the dream, a heightening and blending of the visual, auditory, and kinesthetic senses. For example, Tricia, who had had a near-death experience, described this phenomenon: "I was sitting next to a magical stream. The stream was made of rippling waves of brilliant color. The stream flowed with enchanted sound. If you could hear the stream for even a second, you would probably never feel afraid or angry." Feeling sounds, hearing images and, tasting rhythms are all examples of synesthesia. The ability to experience such a synthesis is described both by poets and by people in mystical or altered states — and is often a marker of visitation and precognitive dreams.

Raymond Moody reported that in near-death experiences, when people encounter their deceased beloveds in the "afterlife," the latter often appear as they did in the prime of their lives. This is often the case in dreams as well.

Finally, in dreams, the beloveds convey very clear messages. Unlike our ordinary dreams, which can be chaotic and unclear, visitation dreams often carry clear and specific messages, as in the two described above.

He Bargained for Fifteen More Years

Bella Mckenzie, an elementary school teacher, shared a story about her father's "premonition" about dying. He was a strict father and rarely showed much affection. He also was not a very spiritual man. And when Bella was seven years old, her father had a heart attack, leaving him dead for almost six minutes. At that time, he did not share what happened to him during those 360 seconds. But he was a changed man. "He was more loving in every way," Bella explained, "and family became the center of his life."

When Bella was a teenager, her father told the family what had happened that day he died: He had gone through a tunnel, seen a bright light, and communicated telepathically with a wise, loving presence. In the conversation, her father had bargained with the voice, which he felt was that of God.

He had pleaded with God for fifteen more years, because he had seven children to raise. God agreed, he told his family, on one condition: the man had to live more spiritually and lovingly in the years to come. Bella's father had agreed.

He counted off the years until the August before the completion of his fifteen years. "That September he died. Could it be that it was a self-fulfilling prophecy? I don't think so," Bella told me. "I believe strongly that my dad had an encounter with God — and that his premonition was based on some kind of real encounter when he died and then came back."

I Had a Feeling

Not only do our loved ones have premonitions about their own dying, but also family members and friends can feel something is wrong. They may experience symptoms, such as an anxiety attack, or problems breathing, only to find out later that someone they loved had just died. The following story illustrates this.

Mark was visiting with his friend Pete, who lived about seven miles from Mark's parents' home. Mark was suddenly overcome by anxiety, and he told Pete that he had to head back home to see his family. He had no idea why, but he drove extremely quickly. At the same time, his sister called Pete's to tell him that Mark should come home immediately. Minutes later, as Mark approached the house, the anxiety lifted. As he turned the corner, he saw an ambulance in the driveway and his father lying there. A short time later at the hospital, his father was pronounced dead. "It was as if my father had called me or got me to come, like he summoned me for help."

Under the Skin

Terri Segal, whose dream of her brother Duffy was described above, began to experience powerful surges of energy after his death. Like Mark, she felt a connection to her beloved at the time of his death and afterward that was primarily kinesthetic, felt in her body.

Duffy left this world on July 24, 2014. I can say I knew that morning at a "just under the skin" level that he was gone. I had just gotten into bed when I suddenly felt a thud or more like a shove against my back. It registered just below consciousness as I thought, "That is strange," and went to sleep. It turns out that the moment I felt the shove was just around the time he passed.

On a September night I had my first "energy experience." Two months after Duffy passed, I came home one night after work heartsick and tired. I lay on my bed with my arms out and palms up. I was crying and wondering, How do I go on? How do I accept this? I spontaneously asked if he would like to visit me. I said, "Duffy I love you and miss you; I am so sorry I could not save you. Can you forgive me and would you please visit with me?" I was given an answer.

Within seconds, a sensation of rolling energy came into my right palm. I felt several minutes of waves of energy, pulsing, circling, stroking my palm and forearm. It seemed he was sending gentle, playful and strong energy to show me that he still exists in a different form. The thought came to me: "I am not gone, only existing on a different level and I will always be in your heart, loving you and connected to you, sister."

"It's you, Duffy, I can feel you!" I asked if it was really him. I asked for him to squeeze my hand. I felt a spark on my fingertips and a pressure all around my forearm and hand.

Now, I am a rational woman, a professional. Still, this was a stretch for even my level of openness and curiosity. I briefly thought to myself: Am I having a hallucination, some form of grief psychosis?

Amazingly, I have felt the presence of this energy every day now, at least twice a day, since September 2014. Every day I ask for him to visit. Every day I have felt this energy, with slight variations, but always most strongly on my right arm and palm. I keep asking for these experiences and writing about them.

Doorbells, Alarms, and Lightbulbs

Among the most common of synchronicities are those related to electricity. I received many accounts of people who have received messages at the time of someone's death, or soon after, that are communicated with the help of electricity — doorbells, alarms, and lightbulbs.

Deirdre, a social worker, shared with me a story about her fortieth birthday. She had invited her friend Richard over to celebrate. While they were drinking wine before dinner, the doorbell began to ring. Deirdre went to get the front door, but no one was there. The ringing would not stop. The bell just kept ringing and ringing, and this had never happened before. Richard, who was a contractor, told her it was a short; but even after he tinkered with it, it continued to ring. That next morning, Deirdre received the news that a very good friend living outside of the country had died suddenly from a rare form of cancer, which she had not known he had. The friend had passed away in the half hour before her doorbell began ringing. "How do you explain that?" she asked me.

Another electrical occurrence made good on a wife's promise to her husband. Their son, Thomas, submitted this story. A few days after Thomas's mother died, his father was lying in bed thinking of his dearly missed wife. He recalled that they had once agreed that whoever died first would give the other some kind of message to convey that there was an afterlife. Just as this thought crossed his mind, there was a large boom in the house. Thomas was concerned that his father had fallen or hurt himself, so he ran upstairs. There was glass everywhere. The globe over the lightbulb in his mother's old sewing room had exploded. However, the lightbulb inside was untouched and still worked. His father told him, "I quietly asked your mom if she was going to give me a sign of life after death, then the globe exploded..." The light had been there for well over twenty years and the ring and screws were intact.

Winn told me that she thought a smoke alarm beeping out of control was communication from her beloved Coleman. The talented Coleman had played in a band called Smoke.

> I realized the first night that it was Coleman, and that he was beeping the smoke alarm. I figured out pretty quickly that it was not a mechanical malfunction. I got out of bed and went out and started talking to him. The beeping stopped until the next night, when he came back at four-ish. A few days later, my brother Rob walked in with his family, and the smoke alarm beeped just once. I told Rob I thought it was Coleman, but he was in motion to disconnect it while chuckling at my comment. Then he said, "How odd; the battery seems fine." We got another beep or two over the next hour, and then a final beep in tandem with the alarm on the other side of the room.

Renee had a series of experiences related to the death of her mother that included many of the elements introduced earlier: a palpable energetic presence, strange occurrences with electricity, and personal and meaningful objects apparently acting as conveyors of messages from beyond. She wrote:

When they [members of Renee's family] arrived around 8:30, the director of the crematorium informed them that the electricity for the entire block was out, and therefore it was impossible for Mom's cremation to take place that day. We had been informed earlier that they never did cremations on the weekend. I guess Mom had other plans. She was cremated on a Saturday.

A little later on the same Friday, in Petaluma [California], I was working on the computer in my office when I tried to turn on the overhead light. The overhead light has four bulbs in it. It wouldn't turn on. We had never had electrical problems in my office before. I had my husband, Steve, come out to try to fix it. He tried a number of things to no avail. We then left to take a walk. When we returned, the box containing some of Mom's belongings that I had mailed to myself a few days earlier was sitting on the porch. I brought it in and then went back to my office. The overhead light was now on. The next evening, we were sitting around the dining room table when we saw this same light in my office blinking on and off, on and off, a number of times.

I called my brother, Sean, in Portland [Oregon] to report these strange electrical occurrences. He informed me that when he had returned to his photography studio, there had been an electrical surge that had blown out several pieces of equipment.

Back in Petaluma a couple of days later, I was sitting in my office late at night talking with my daughter, Bryn, about Mom. I was also sitting in front of my computer waiting for the first draft of Mom's obituary to come in from Sean via email. Suddenly, all the lights went out. I checked my watch. It was 10:55. I went out onto the street and realized that all the lights on the entire street, 12 blocks down to the river, were dark. Exactly two hours later, all the lights came on again. The next morning I checked my email. Sean's email with the draft of Mom's obituary had come in the night before. It was time-stamped 10:55 — the exact time that the electricity had gone out.

High-Tech Talking

Accounts of communication from the dying and the dead have been recorded throughout time and cultures. Our modern-day accounts now include this new twist: text messages. The following account sent to me by Debbie Ribar comes from her sister-in-law Joanne Moylan Aubé:

> My father passed away last January while I was sitting outside with my mom (miles from the assisted-living facility). My brother was by Dad's side at this time, because Dad was breathing heavily and nearing the end of his life. He was not conscious. While I was sitting peacefully in my brother's backyard, my iPhone made a noise similar to Siri's beeping response. I looked at the phone and saw a text, which showed up as though I had written it. It said, "Was leaving heavily might be just wind and downy might be ready to go bad that I like pneumonia now maybe get tired I'm down I'm going to be around anymore."
>
> I freaked out and called my brother, who was as shocked as I was by this message. After reading it over and over, I determined it meant: "I am breathing heavily now

and might be winding down. Might be ready to go now. Feels like pneumonia. Maybe getting tired. I'm down and am not going to be around anymore."

My dad has never texted or understood iPhones or technology and was clearly not conscious in the sense that we know. I don't know if he had terrestrial help, or if it was just that his energy was able to convey a message to me. His name was Raymond Aubé.

A grieving husband, Ka Lok, received a mysterious text message from a taxicab company after his wife lost consciousness following multiple strokes. The message said that the taxi he requested had arrived at his workplace, and that the driver didn't see anyone. Ka Lok had not requested a taxi, since he always drove to his office at 95 Plenty Road. However, his wife, Elizabeth, used to sometimes take a taxi from her workplace. At that hour, which was midnight, while his wife was unconscious, there would be no reason to get a taxi home. Ka Lok told me, "As a matter of fact, that night before she lost consciousness, she said she wanted to go home. I am convinced that she is now home, and that her life goes on in the afterlife."

When Ka Lok emailed me his account, he sent a photo of the cab company's text message: "The driver we sent has indicated that they could not find you at 95 Plenty Road. If you still need a cab at this address, reply yes."

There could, perhaps, be other explanations. And for many of the accounts, there are other explanations, because they represent synchronicities. And synchronicity appears, in most cases, to be one of the defining characteristics of communications that people experience as being sent from across the threshold. This text message from the taxi company, too, could be explained in a number of ways; however, it is hard to escape the poignancy of these "coincidences."

Synchronicities in Nature

Many people told me that different animals appeared soon after the deaths of their loved ones. A common theme is the appearance of birds and butterflies who maintain close contact much longer than would normally be expected. Common were stories of birds that seemed to hover at windows and peer in for extended periods of time.

Rich Shlicht explained that he went for a walk soon after the passing of his mother, thinking to himself how he wished she would give him some sign of an afterlife. Soon after, a sparrow appeared and walked with him on the path, close to his heel, without fear, for over an hour. The bird then followed him home and sat on his bedroom windowsill, where it remained for minutes, as if to say, "I am here, son. All is well."

Birds were the most common species in these accounts, but I also heard stories of butterflies, dogs, and cats. "Within a couple of minutes of Mom's passing, we heard a cat meowing very loudly outside in the courtyard. It went on for a long time. I hadn't seen or heard a cat in the days before or after Mom's death." Interestingly enough, these species also appeared in the visions of the dying. There were no other animals in my sample of deathbed or after-death communication.

Personal Possessions

Common also are stories about personal possessions that seem to carry messages from the dying. Kaye Elliott shared this story about a special wooden box:

> My daughter was friendly with a young woman of twenty-three called Ruth, who was attending a development circle run by the Spiritualist Church in an effort to develop her

psychic gifts. She offered to try to contact my mother and later turned up with a drawing of a box made of carved wood, which had a lip inside and was decorated with a pattern of white diamonds. It contained a piece of paper, some jewelry, and some buttons. She said my mother was of stocky build and her middle name could be Emma. In fact, she was of stocky build but her middle name was Ethel.

I had no knowledge of such a box, my mother had lived fifty miles away, and Ruth had never met her or visited her house. I put the matter out of my mind. However, when clearing out my mother's bungalow some days later, my daughter suddenly said, "Look, Mum," and handed me a carved wooden box that had a pattern of white diamonds on the top of it (arranged slightly differently from those in the drawing) and contained exactly what Ruth had said. There was nothing written on the piece of paper. Years before, my mother and I had been discussing whether we thought there was life after death, and I made her promise to contact me if she died before I did. I can think of no logical explanation of this occurrence, and neither can my rather skeptical husband, which is amazing.

As in the preceding examples, synchronicities are closely connected to the interests or themes of the person's life, as are the metaphors and symbols that appear in the language of our final days. The following story from a photographer's sister clearly illustrates this.

Renee's brother Sean was a professional photographer, and he died from lung cancer at age forty-eight. He had a son, and months after his father's death the boy was getting ready to celebrate his eleventh birthday. The year before, Eugenia, who was Renee and Sean's mother, had also died. As Renee drove home from work on her nephew's birthday, she imagined a conversation with her mother and brother, asking that they join the family for dinner in some way.

Moments after the family members were all seated at the table, they heard a large crash upstairs. Renee ran upstairs to see what had happened.

One of the photographs on a shelf in her hallway had fallen on the floor, and the metal frame and two glass pieces were now disassembled on the floor. The photo was facedown. Renee turned it over. It was a picture of her mother and brother. Of the thirty-plus photos in her hallway, this was the only one of Sean, and it happened to include his mother, Eugenia. In the ten years that Renee had had photos in the hallway, no frame had ever fallen. She brought the photo to the dining table as a symbolic way of bringing everyone together again.

They're Playing Our Song

Many people shared accounts of a signature song that appeared at poignant times and places. One example of this comes from Kathleen Stiles:

> "Morning Has Broken" was one of Bob's favorite songs. We sang it at an Easter church service in Bhutan and many other times. On the night before he passed, he was pretty much in a coma, unable to speak. One of his close friends was in the room with him. I said, "We are going to sing for you." He responded, "La, la, la" (which he often said). We sang "Morning Has Broken" to him and played the Cat Stevens version as well on an iPhone. The next morning, a friend who played the harp for hospice patients called. She didn't know Bob had passed, but said she woke up feeling she should come and play the song for him.
>
> A few months after Bob passed over, I was at work at an

English-language school for international students, where I teach. I was missing Bob a lot. I opened a dictionary, and out fell an old mimeographed copy of the words to "Morning Has Broken." I had never seen anything like that paper before, and haven't since. No such old machine existed in the school at the time. A little over a year and a half later, I went to a past-life regression therapist/medium who plays music to help people get into an open state. The first song played was an instrumental version of "Morning Has Broken." I asked her if she always played the same music. She said no, but that she plays the song she is led to play. Even last Sunday, I had another experience with this song. I went to hear medium Hollister Rand speak and give messages at the Spiritualist Church in Santa Barbara. I told Bob it would be good to hear from him there, even though I feel I hear from him often on my own. I didn't get a spoken message from the medium, but the first hymn we sang was "Morning Has Broken."

Gestalt of Synchronicities

Elaine Unell, a retired teacher of gifted education, shared the co-incidences that occurred before and after her husband's death. The synchronicities created a gestalt that formed a sustained narrative not unlike the metaphorical and symbolic narratives we see in the language of the dying. Some of the synchronicities seem trivial, and others more dramatic; however, the combined effect throughout the days leading to and after her husband's death were deeply meaningful and comforting to Elaine.

Throughout her husband's illness, the number 18 became increasingly significant. Elaine, who is Jewish, explained, "The Jewish word for 18, Chai, means 'life,' so when he was admitted to the cardiac critical care unit and placed in room 18, I took it as a sign of hope." When a friend asked what his favorite number was, so he could put it on a Cardinals Jersey for him, Ron mouthed "18." Ron died on September 18 (9/18). As a lifelong golfer, Ron typically would play either 9 or 18 holes. For about six months on the eighteenth of every month, it seemed to Elaine that she was getting "signs from him," whether this entailed finding money, seeing and feeling him in dreams, or other small synchronicities.

However, these numerical synchronicities were just the beginning. Before his death, Elaine would sit in the hospital with him and entertain herself with an iPad game called Cryptograms. Each letter is assigned a different letter to represent it, and then a quote is spelled out using the assigned letters. The solver uses logic and reasoning to determine what each letter stands for and eventually figures out what the quote is. The quotes are randomly selected from all genres and time periods. At this particular time, the quote Elaine was solving happened to be by Socrates. Elaine sent me a screenshot of the cryptogram. She had completed all the letters except one. The cryptogram read, "The hour of departure has arrived, and we go our ways — I to die, and you to live. Which is better god only — nows."

The *k* that belongs in *knows* was never solved, but it gave the impression that it should be read "now," lending it a sense of immediacy, or at least giving it a double meaning.

"After seeing this I felt sickened," Elaine explained to me. "I felt as though I were getting a message from Source telling me he was going to die. But I could not, would not, let that be true yet. However, the feeling of nearing the end was pervasive, and the quote from Cryptogram was a haunting premonition of this."

In the week following, Elaine's husband died twice and returned to fight courageously. Machines kept him breathing and the blood pumping through his body while he had a dozen surgeries over the next two and a half months. Elaine had hoped that he would be able to have a heart transplant, but infection in his chest cavity kept him off the heart transplant list. She explained, "The choice was to let him go on living in this horrible, painful, and imprisoned mechanical manner, or to let go of his body and release his soul from its human form. This [release] is what it became very clear that he wanted, probably sooner than we who loved him wanted to accept. He was brave enough to give us our hopes for his recovery, but the doctors assured us that it was time to let him go." On September 18, 2014, his wife and closest loved ones gathered around him, and at 7:32 PM, as they watched a sadly beautiful sunset out his window, he took his last breath.

As Elaine looked out at the horizon, she was struck by what she saw. The sun was sinking beneath the skyscrapers in the distance, and the sky was layered in yellows, oranges, and purples. The view from his hospital window was beautiful and comforting. Coincidentally (or perhaps in retrospect, a foreshadowing), in May 2014, just before her husband had become ill, she had been taking an oil painting class. Looking at some photos, she had been having trouble deciding what to paint. Among the images she perused was a photo of her husband and herself on a cruise, with the sunset behind them. Elaine told me, "Something kept pulling me back to that photo. In the photo we were looking at the camera, but I decided to paint us in silhouette and turned us around as though we were looking out at the sunset." As Elaine regarded the final scene out the window of his hospital room on the night he died, she was struck by how eerily reminiscent the view in front of her was of that last painting.

Over the years, Elaine has developed the practice of automatic writing and has received many messages that seem to come from the "other side." It has been her experience with others who have passed that the best communications started two weeks after their passing. Given that, two weeks after Ron died she began asking for messages from him. When she inquired about the Cryptogram message, these were the words that emerged:

Elaine, when you received that message, I also received it. We were both told at the same time in different ways. I heard a voice in my head that told me just those words, and I was pretty sure that it meant I was to die, but I didn't want to believe it. You also received that message and did not want to believe it, but it was true, and now I know and I can tell you that what I have over here is better than life as a human form. We all need to endure the human life to learn and grow for our soul development, but on this side there is so much more than you know over there. All is well and as it should be. Do not feel bad for me. Just live your life as happily as you can. Continue on your good path, and you will arrive here when the time is right. You are loved. Ron.

Automatic Writing

As was true for Elaine, several people I interviewed experienced messages from their beloveds by means of automatic writing. Terri Daniel, in her book *A Swan in Heaven*, talks about the afterlife messages she received from her teenage son, who communicated telepathically with her after his death. Danny died at age sixteen after struggling with a degenerative disorder that had begun when he was an active, healthy seven-year-old, and which had eventually transformed him into a wheelchair-bound teenager who wore diapers, was unable to talk, and could not use his hands. He was completely nonverbal during the last years of his life, but within an hour after his death he began "speaking" to his mother. Terri explained that, as Danny lost his ability to speak, her telepathic abilities increased, and that this ability continued after he died.

About fourteen days after my father passed away, I awoke one morning to hear his voice as clearly as I had while he was alive. He said, "Please write this poem down and give it to your mother." My

father, a poet, recited this first poem of what was to be over thirty
poems in the course of two years:

For I Will Always Hear You

Even in heaven
no light shines
as brightly as Susan.

The cosmos sings for you
as the days pass,
and I become the mountains
with their longing for spring
after long snowy winters.

We are wed always,
like boat to harbor,
even as I sail out
to this vast sea of galaxy;

you are always mine, beloved
Susan,
and the poems call out to you beyond
the seams of angels
to your tattered tears.

Do not cry too long.
Let that laughter of your love
illuminate
the skies, for I
will always

hear you.

While these poems gave my mother great comfort in her time of grief, I was somewhat uncomfortable with them at first. I did not want to deceive my mother if they were just products of my imagination. I was mystified by the presence of this language — but also drawn into its beauty and its wisdom. Whose voice was it? My father's? Mine? The voice of the collective unconscious? Although the poems were a mystery to me, I wrote down the words — as it seemed, then, a natural extension of all those weeks spent sitting beside him and writing down his last utterances.

For me, transcribing his final words offered one way to step into my father's world and follow him beyond, from where his poems later came. As I did so, I felt what the great composer Johann Sebastian Bach had expressed in his last words to his wife: "Don't cry for me, I am going where music is born."

I had never imagined that as my father was dying I could ever feel so close to him, and to Source — closer than ever in those last days and hours. And what surprises me now is that his voice and his presence are still with me, in ways I had never imagined possible, especially given that my father was so skeptical. This connection began while he was dying and I was tracking his dying words.

Shared Death Experiences

One of the strongest memories I have of my father's final weeks was of waking up in the middle of the night in my home, which was an hour's drive away from him. I looked at the digital clock with its red numbers glowing in the darkness; it read 3:15. I felt as if the room were crowded with people. I whispered to my husband, "Do you feel something?" Then I saw swirls of energy and felt as if my grandmothers were there. "I think my dad might be dying now." I said, "Something is going on."

"Your mom will call you if anything is going on...Go back to sleep."

When I came to visit my father the next day, I asked my mother how everything was going. She said, "Strangest thing. Your father woke up at 3:15 and started talking about all the people in the room. He said something about the room being so crowded and he did not have time to talk to all those people." How remarkable! It was as if in some way he and I were sharing an experience outside of the normal time and place. I came to learn that an experience like this is called a *shared death experience*, a term coined by Raymond Moody.

My father and I were attuned to one another in that experience. And because of that attunement, hearing his voice reciting poems to me after he died felt very natural to me. Why some of us are attuned to our beloved during the dying process — and even afterward — is a mystery, one that William Peters, a marriage and family therapist who founded the Shared Crossings Project, has addressed in his workshops.

Shared Crossings works with families and individuals to teach them about the profound and healing experiences possible throughout the dying process — with a special focus on how people can gain greater alignment with those they love as they cross the threshold. Peters explained to me that as we sit with the dying, we can often have profound spiritual experiences. Families and friends may witness unique changes in the room of the person who is dying — for example, they may feel or see unusual light, heat, mist, or other things, or they may experience telepathic communication with a loved one or feel the presence of the unseen in the room.

As many have expressed in this chapter, through the dying process we can experience strong connection not only to our beloveds but also to Source. Peters explained that there is a vortex of energy associated with death and dying, not unlike the charged energy many people feel in a room where a child has just been born. He talked about the powerful energy of that vortex, and how, often, those who learn to attune themselves to the energies of death and dying not only create deeper relationships with their loved ones but also gain greater spiritual insight and understanding that can ameliorate the grief and fear associated with the end of life. Peters explained that this process of alignment allows beloveds to "step into the vortex that appears to open as people die." This was clearly my experience and the experience of so many others who shared their words with me and stories of their loved ones' final days, even of the moments during and after death.

Many I interviewed shared with me their knowledge that someone they loved, and who had died, was still with them. These stories came from people of all walks of life who felt that the after-death communication elevated their spirits and gave them a deeper connection to the Divine and to those they loved. If communications like these were only the result of imagination, would they have such a profound ability to console us, uplift us, and offer such insight and wisdom? And would we see so many synchronicities, so many shared experiences while miles and hours apart?

CONCLUSION

Hearing Is Healing
A Few Final Words

> Do you hear that music? It is so beautiful!
> It is the most beautiful thing I have ever heard.
> Bye-bye.
> — *Claire, Final Words Project participant,*
> *to her grown children a few hours before dying*

What might be the view from the threshold? And what words will you say as you look out upon it? All of us will someday utter, think, or dream our final words. And most of us will one day be at the bedside of someone else who will do so. For those of us who are living, what exists beyond the threshold is a mystery — just as it was to all of those who came before us.

Unique and Compelling Accounts

In *Words at the Threshold*, I discuss the patterns that I found in the more than fifteen hundred utterances recorded in the Final Words Project. For the most part, I found clustered patterns and themes, with a few fascinating exceptions. These exceptions come from reliable sources, so the question is, Why did so few emerge through the research? Nevertheless, they bear mentioning here, because they open up the possibility of further inquiry into, and greater support for, the notion of the survival of consciousness, particularly in regard to past lives.

Reincarnation emerges repeatedly in the accounts of those who have had near-death experiences, but only traces of it appear in transcripts of the Final Words Project. This account sent to me by Charles Griffin, author of *Darwin Plus!*, was the most compelling:

> The closest I have come to direct evidence for reincarnation came during a conversation with a Congregationalist minister, who told me he had many times witnessed dying people claiming to see "the light" before finally passing away. He had also recently officiated at the deathbed of a twenty-two-year-old man. As he began to fade, the young man said, apropos of nothing, "We agreed on twenty-two years this time." The minister asked the obvious question: "Agreed with whom?" But the young man would say no more and slipped into unconsciousness. The minister was quite sure that "this time" implied "other times," which could only mean "other lives." This was a shock for the good Christian minister, as was the "agreement" and the "twenty-two years."

Add to this the several cases in which people described dying loved ones speaking the languages of their childhood or homeland. A handful of submissions to the Final Words Project involved individuals who spoke the foreign language of their childhood, even if decades had passed since the person had spoken it. Most compelling of these examples was an email I received from Melissa: "My mother told me about her sister who died when she was only ten. When she was dying, she pointed behind my mother and said, 'Look at that handsome man behind you!' Then she started speaking in another language that no one recognized."

Many intriguing questions remain about language, cognition, and consciousness at the end of life. Among them are questions that concern a cross-linguistic analysis of final words. Are some of the patterns that I have discussed in *Words at the Threshold* specific solely to English? Will we see the same kinds of patterns in other languages?

Maggie La Tourelle, the author of *The Gift of Alzheimer's*, discerned many similarities in the patterns of speech of her mother, who had Alzheimer's disease, and those of the individuals whose words were recorded in the Final Words Project. Maggie wrote me an email suggesting that perhaps Alzheimer's is a kind of protracted dying process in which the same shifts of language appear, but over a longer period of time. Research into the parallels between end-of-life language and the language of Alzheimer's may prove to be an area of fruitful investigation, as may research into the language of autism, mental illness, and altered states. Language at the threshold of human experience in a variety of contexts would offer many opportunities to better understand who we are and what consciousness is.

Tracking the Path of Final Words

Judging from the informal research of the Final Words Project, it appears that who we are in life is who we are in death; we cross the threshold with the symbols, metaphors, and meanings of our life narrative and enter into another dimension, or way of seeing, as our language gives way to increasingly figurative and nonsensical expression.

By honoring the language of the end of life — including the language that is unintelligible to us — we can better honor those we love in their final days and ultimately better understand the cognitive processes associated with dying. As we do, we will have deeper relationships with them and more meaningful memories, as well as possible answers to our inquiries about the afterlife.

Words at the Threshold shows that writing down our loved one's final words can lead to insight and a sense of attunement with that person. Through examples of metaphors of the momentous, the dying often let us know that death is near — by speaking of an important occasion or momentous moment that is arriving, often using symbols connected to their lives. We also hear metaphors associated with traveling or leaving — and the data indicate that these metaphors usually have outside agency. That is, generally, dying people speak of awaiting vehicles of transportation — something outside of them takes them away.

The informal research of the Final Words Project, and the more rigorous research undertaken in decades past and present, indicates that people see and communicate with those who have died before them. And when they do so, a deep peace often accompanies these visions and visitations, which are usually different from the hallucinations associated with medications.

My hope is that *Words at the Threshold* has inspired you to see how the language at the end of life may be more than simply a confusing "word salad." In many cases, it may be that the language forms we find are more complex than those of ordinary healthy people. We may hear sophisticated metaphors and symbols much like the ones recorded by one individual: "He struggled to speak even as he was losing language, and his sentences came out slowly, like loosely strung poetry. He called the lamp by his bedside the 'thing...connected...to sun.' He wondered how he could be in Wednesday while I was in Tuesday."

The images that emerge in the voices of the dying are often consistent with the speakers' personalities and life stories, and these images sometimes evolve over days or even weeks in sustained narratives. We may find fascinating and complex repetition, such as "so much so in sorrow" or "how much wider does this wider go?" We may hear paradoxical speech or hybrid language in which it appears the person we love is standing between two worlds, such as when someone asks for his glasses in order to have a better view of the landscape unfolding before him. We may see remarkable surges of clarity just as it seems that our loved one is fading permanently into the dark. These are some of the remarkable qualities of the language of the dying that you may discover when you are sitting bedside or find yourself at the threshold of life. You may have been, or perhaps someday will be, witness to sudden lucidity.

We may hear words of elevated or unique awareness or requests for forgiveness and reconciliation — or we may have shared death experiences, in which we ourselves seem to be taken out of the ordinary restrictions of time and place and seem to become more fully aligned with our loved one. Some of us may have unusual telepathic or symbolic communications that are different from what we have experienced before. Others may notice the many ways our loved ones tell us that death is near, such as my father's announcement that the angels told him there were only three days left.

It appears that as we approach death, the areas in our brain associated with literal thought and language produce a new way of speaking and thinking. The shift may represent a larger movement away from this dimension to another — or at least to another way of thinking, feeling, and being. When we look at the utterances of the dying, we see that the language often forms a continuum, and this continuum appears to correlate with brain function. The continuum spans literal, figurative, and unintelligible language — and then finally nonverbal and even telepathic communication. Literal language is language of ordinary reality, the five senses; it is purposeful and intelligible language. Brain scans reveal that literal language such as "that chair over there has four brown legs and a white cushion" engages the left hemisphere. The left hemisphere houses the regions that are traditionally considered the speech centers.

However, the results are different when people speak metaphorically. A sentence such as "the chair over there looks like a koala bear" engages both the left and the right brain hemispheres. The right hemisphere has traditionally been associated with the more ineffable aspects of life: music, visual art, and spirituality. Metaphors appear to be a bridge between the two hemispheres and perhaps two different states of being.

Recent and early findings into nonsense reveal it may be associated with parts of the brain not associated with purposeful language, that it might be more closely related to music and mystical states. Speaking nonsense may be more like music, since it relies so heavily on the rhythms and sounds of language rather than its meanings. It appears that the very reductions we see in brain function at the end of life may correlate both to nonsensical language and to transpersonal and mystical states.

A New Transcendental Sense

Perhaps, then, we are hardwired for transcendent experience at the end of life. Many survivors of near-death experiences have said that when they died, they entered a world with no space or time. The language of the dying also seems to indicate changes in orientation. Recall the phrases indicating movement and travel — such as "help me down from here" — that came from people who were relatively motionless in bed. The language seems to indicate that people's perception of themselves in space shifts significantly; and accordingly, so does their use of prepositions (those small words that describe position).

As we die, most of us move away from the sense-ical language of literal reality and toward a more non-sense-ical, nonsensory, or even multisensory awareness. The language patterns of those who have had near-death experiences track a very similar trajectory.

This new awareness may relate to what Kenneth Ring and Sharon Cooper, authors of *Mindsight*, call "transcendental awareness." They coined this term when researching the near-death experiences and out-of-body experiences (OBEs) of the blind. The majority of the participants in the study — even those who had been blind since birth — described being able to see during their OBEs and NDEs.

In some cases, participants described details such as the color and patterns of a doctor's tie, the snowfall outside the window, or the physical traits of specific medical personnel, family members, and their own bodies "below." The details were corroborated by others during the research. The participants explained that during their OBEs and NDEs, they could see as they had never seen before in waking life or in dreams.

As Ring and Cooper explored the participants' notion of seeing during these experiences, they discovered that the participants' perceptions were actually synesthetic. The blind NDEers in the study described seeing, hearing, and feeling all at once, and they called this kind of perception "transcendental awareness." It is possible, then, that as we die we move away from our usual sensory awareness to something different — something that actually includes all the senses at once.

This integrated perception may also relate to the findings Madelaine Lawrence discusses in her book *In a World of Their Own.* Coma survivors reported experiencing telepathic communication, continued sensory and energetic awareness, and heightened emotional attunement. Lawrence reports that as people's physical functioning decreases, they frequently experience increased extrasensory perception and awareness.

Perhaps the changes in language that we see at the end of life are part of the process of developing a new sense — not nonsense. This new sense is the transcendental awareness described by the participants in Ring and Cooper's study and other near-death and out-of-body experiencers. Is there another dimension, a *new* transcendental *sense*? Those who have died and returned tell us they have no doubt that something exists beyond the threshold. Final words may indeed be the tracks in the sand that will lead us to better understand the pathways traveled by the dying.

Hearing Is Healing

My hope is that *Words at the Threshold* offers insight into the sometimes incomprehensible utterances of those at the end of life, and that it will give you a vocabulary for speaking not only about dying but also about consciousness. As we bear witness to the language of the dying, we are invited to journey with our beloveds into new territory.

When you sit beside the dying, open your heart.

And remember that hearing is healing. As you listen closely, you may find that your beloveds offer you insight and reassurance — even in words that may, upon first hearing them, be puzzling.

The more at ease we are with the language of the threshold, the greater comfort we can bring to those who are dying and to all those dear to our beloveds.

I asked Stephen Jones, of Hospice of Santa Barbara, if he would share some of his wisdom about communicating with those at the threshold. He wrote me to say, "The dying need us to be exceptional listeners in order to be understood. The language of the dying is comprehended best when taken in through the gill of our hearts. Each syllable is sacred and should be received as a gift."

Indeed, they were received.

And here, my dear father, they are returned to you, multiplied.

Acknowledgments

I t takes a village to birth a book.

This book was conceived with the loving support of many, including William Taegel, Judith Yost, Jim Garrison, and Jim Van Overshelde, who offered an approach to academics that did not exclude the life of the spirit, and who introduced me to Raymond Moody. Carolyn Atkinson's wise, measured input as my dissertation adviser guided this work in many more ways than she might ever have imagined.

Special thanks to Geoffrey Leigh, whose music and research opened new pathways in my life and in my work. From the project's very early days, Claire Joy validated the longing in my heart to better understand my father's last words, kept in touch with me across distances, and encouraged me to walk the proposal for this book into the offices of New World Library.

I am deeply grateful also to those who supported the book through its most fragile, embryonic stages. Erica Goldblatt Hyatt of Bryn Athyn College opened her academic home to me, extended other kindnesses as well, and shared her impassioned energy and insights. I am also deeply appreciative of the administration and faculty of Bryn Athyn College for all they did to support research into the communications of the dying. Thanks to Amy Cavanaugh, who was among the first to nourish the idea of the Final Words Project, and who traveled miles, several times, to sit with me and offer words of wisdom. Isabelle Chauffeton Saavedra supported this research in so many ways—large and small.

With tender generosity, Winn Mallard shared her father's last words with me, and her insights into death, dying, and spirit fueled my work. I will be forever grateful for her kindness, especially as I was a newcomer to Georgia. I offer my gratitude as well to other amazing women of Athens, Georgia: Shannon Willis, Elizabeth Alder, Ellen Bleier, and Jill Hartmann-Roberts, who welcomed me with such big hearts and open arms, and especially Kelli McConnell, who shared in my wonder of those magnificent owls.

My appreciation goes to those whose words and accounts are incorporated into *Words at the Threshold*, including the researchers and health-care providers whose commitment to the dying and their families profoundly moved me.

Thanks to Georgia Hughes of New World Library and copyeditor Bonita Hurd. Their expert suggestions deeply honored my voice and ideas. Appreciation also goes to the folks at California Library Literacy Services, including Linda Sakamoto-Jahnke, Ben Ocón, Lisa Dale, Carol Stults, Donya Sultani, Karen Gardner, and others who made it possible logistically for this book to be written.

Finally, I thank those closest to me who have been there throughout the book's emergence into life. Enduring love to my mother, Susan, and my husband, John — both of whom never questioned me as I left behind a secure job and life in California to move to Georgia to pursue research into final words. I greatly appreciate my mother's steadfast support and her ability to stay amazed no matter what life brings. This book would never have been written without my husband's great sense of humor, overflowing hugs, belief in the importance of inquiry, and willingness to live humbly. Great gratitude goes to my daughter, Eliana, who, at age eighteen, had the courage to live on her own on the West Coast as I moved to the East. I am so grateful for the encouragement she offered as I set out to investigate the questions that arose in response to her grandfather's final conversations. Huge gratitude to my dear friends Renee Kirk and Kevin Nierman: our friendships have endured decades and losses. Their insights, reflections, and love have informed my life and this book.

And of course, great gratitude goes to Raymond Moody and his wife, Cheryl, who opened their doors and hearts to me as we shared a joy for language and fascination in the world that lives at the threshold.

And lastly, thank you to my father, and all the ancestors, who taught me that the widening portal takes life away but also gives rise to it. My father's memory and that of my grandparents guided and supported this work.

All of these people, living and in Spirit, are among those in the village who made *Words at the Threshold* possible. There are many others, I am sure, who go unnamed. I offer my love and deepest gratitude to all of them.

Notes

Chapter One: Transcribing the Mystery

Page 10 *"That week before Roger passed"*: Chris Jones, "The Death of Roger Ebert," *Esquire*, December 24, 2013, 3.

Page 11 *"I've come to appreciate the difficulty"*: Ray Robinson, comp., *Famous Last Words: Fond Farewells, Deathbed Diatribes, and Exclamations upon Expiration* (New York: Workman, 2003), x.

Page 14 *"What is the answer?"*: Elizabeth Sprigge, *Gertrude Stein: Her Life, Her Work* (New York: Harper and Bros., 1957), 265.

Page 18 *Bandler and Grinder discovered*: Richard Bandler and John Grinder, *The Structure of Magic I: A Book about Language and Therapy* (Palo Alto, CA: Science and Behavior Books, 1975), 23. Bandler and Grinder developed neurolinguistic programming, which has been criticized for its poorly researched and unscientific approach; however, their model for building rapport through matching representational systems has been effectively applied in psychology, advertising, and education.

Chapter Two: No Words for It

Page 27 *"Previous brain-imaging research"*: Tori Rodriguez, "Study: Metaphors Can Make Up Your Mind," Salon.com, December 10, 2013,

www.salon.com/2013/12/10/study_metaphors_can_make_up_your
_mind_partner/. This article originally appeared in *Scientific American*.

Page 28 *"the mind shifts from an intelligible dimension"*: Raymond Moody,
"Making Sense of Nonsense" (unpublished manuscript, 2013), 36.

Page 34 *"Now, there is a real problem for me"*: Raymond Moody, *Life After
Life* (Covington, GA: Mockingbird Books, 1975), 34.

Page 35 *"special effects of language"*: Moody, "Making Sense of Nonsense," 90.

Page 36 *Of those, 80 percent described*: Kenneth Ring and Sharon Cooper,
Mindsight (Palo Alto, CA: William James Center for Consciousness
Studies at the Institute of Transpersonal Psychology, 1999), 12.

Page 36 *the phrase* life after death *itself violates*: Moody, "Making Sense of
Nonsense," 190.

Page 37 *not only paradoxical but also "nonlinguistic"*: *Conversations beyond
Proof of Heaven*, directed by David Hinshaw (Atlanta, GA: Mudpuppy
Productions, 2013), DVD.

Page 39 *"As the person in the transpersonal experience"*: Madelaine Lawrence,
The Death View Revolution (Hove, UK: White Crow Books, 2014),
195.

Chapter Three: Metaphors of the Momentous

Page 43 *"Then his right hand starts to move"*: Leo Holder, "Remembrances:
The Impromptu Dance," National Public Radio, October 9, 2014,
www.npr.com.

Page 43 *"As I stood in the doorway"*: Douglas C. Smith, *Caregiving* (New
York: Macmillan, 1997), 154–55.

Page 46 *"Each of us has our own set"*: Kelly Bulkeley and Patricia Bulkley,
Dreaming beyond Death (Boston, MA: Beacon Press, 2005), 16.

Page 46 *"the mind is a brittle object"*: George Lakoff, *Metaphors We Live By*
(Chicago: University of Chicago Press, 2003), 27–28.

Page 49 *"battling illness and defeating it"*: Metaphor in End-of-Life Care
project, July 2015, ucrel.lancs.ac.uk/melc/background.php, accessed
May 2016.

Page 50 *"What better picture"*: Robert J. Hoss, email to author, October 29,
2015.

Page 51 *"When a shaman journeys"*: Mandy Peat, email to author, November 4, 2015.

Chapter Four: I Leave You with These Words

Page 56 *The metaphor of death as a journey*: Richard Smith and Nataly Kelly, "Global Attempts to Avoid Talking Directly about Death and Dying," *BMJ Group Blog,* August 16, 2012, blogs.bmj.com/bmj/2012/08/16/richard-smith-and-nataly-kelly-global-attempts-to-avoid-talking-directly-about-death-and-dying.

Page 57 *"I am sailing again at night"*: Kelly Bulkeley and Patricia Bulkley, *Dreaming beyond Death* (Boston, MA: Beacon Press, 2005), 3.

Page 58 *confirmed by a 2014 study*: C. W. Kerr, J. P. Donnelly, S. T. Wright, S. M. Kuszczak, A. Banas, P. C. Grant, and D. L. Luczkiewicz, "End-of-Life Dreams and Visions: A Longitudinal Study of Hospice Patients' Experiences," *Journal of Palliative Medicine* 17, no. 3 (March 2014): 296.

Page 58 *"The first is the calm, direct"*: Van Bronkhorst discussing Marie-Louise von Franz's views based on her clinical work with the dying, in Jeanne Van Bronkhorst, *Dreams at the Threshold* (Woodbury, MN: Llewellyn, 2015), 58.

Page 59 *"It's like this with every crossing"*: Donald Miller, *A Million Miles in a Thousand Years* (Nashville, TN: Thomas Nelson, 2009), 182.

Page 60 *the last words of 407 death row inmates*: Sarah Griffiths, "A Unique Insight into the Minds of Death Row Inmates: Final Statements of the Condemned Reveal Their Last Words Are Usually Positive," *Daily Mail Online,* February 5, 2016, www.dailymail.co.uk/sciencetech/article-3431434/A-unique-insight-minds-death-row-inmates-Final-statements-condemned-reveal-words-usually-POSITIVE.html.

Chapter Five: Repetition, Repetition, Repetition

Page 69 *"Repetition is hypnotic"*: Adam Eason, "Using Repetition in Hypnosis and Hypnotherapy," April 13, 2011, www.adam-eason.com/using-repetition-in-hypnosis-and-hypnotherapy.

Page 73 *"music takes place in time"*: Elizabeth Hellmuth Margulis, "On Repeat: How Music Plays the Mind," undated, www.elizabethmargulis.com/on-repeat, accessed February 20, 2016.

Chapter Six: Nonsense or a New Sense?

Page 90 *"The force of the lightning blast"*: Tony Ciccoria and Jordan Ciccoria, "Getting Comfortable with Near-Death Experience," *Missouri Medicine* (August 2014): 304, emphasis added.

Page 90 *"The body that was on the bed"*: Kenneth Ring and Sharon Cooper, *Mindsight* (Palo Alto, CA: William James Center for Consciousness Studies at the Institute of Transpersonal Psychology, 1999), 38.

Page 92 *"going back and forth across the doorsill"*: Jalal al-Din Rumi, *The Essential Rumi,* trans. Coleman Barks and John Moyne (New York: HarperOne, 2004), 36.

Page 96 *"The next thing I remember was my children"*: Madelaine Lawrence, *In a World of Their Own* (Westport, CT: Bergin and Garvey, 1997), 41.

Page 97 *"dazzling obscurity"*: William James, *William James: Writings, 1902–1910: The Varieties of Religious Experience / Pragmatism / A Pluralistic Universe / The Meaning of Truth / Some Problems of Philosophy / Essays* (New York: Library of America, 1988), 379.

Page 97 *"We delight in nonsense"*: Moody, "Making Sense of Nonsense" (unpublished manuscript, 2013), 7.

Page 98 *what Will Taegel calls "trans-sense"*: Will Taegel, in conversations with Raymond Moody (Greece, October 2010) and Lisa Smartt (May 2012) and "Matters of Life and Death" (lecture, Wisdom University, Anniston, AL, May 14, 2012).

Page 99 *Researchers compared brain scans of individuals*: Ron Philipchalk and Dieter Mueller, "Glossolalia and Temperature Change in the Right and Left Cerebral Hemispheres," *International Journal for the Psychology of Religion* 10, no. 3 (2000): 181.

Page 99 *"Normally when you talk and listen"*: Andrew Newberg and Mark Robert Waldman, *How Enlightenment Changes Your Brain* (London: Hay House, 2016), 110.

Page 100 *those whose psychedelic experiences*: Eben Alexander, "Compelling Studies on Drugs and Consciousness," June 2016, www.ebenalexander.com/compelling-studies-on-drugs-and-consciousness.

Page 100 *"As my neocortex was destroyed"*: Ibid.

Page 102 *he has identified seventy types*: Moody, "Making Sense of Nonsense," 26.

Chapter Seven: Words between the Worlds

Page 105 *"The light showed me the world"*: Kenneth Ring and Evelyn Elsasser, *Lessons from the Light: What We Can Learn from the Near-Death Experience* (Needham, MA: Moment Point Press, 2006), 45.

Page 109 *"At first it looked like there were no serious injuries"*: Paul Luvera, "The Strange Death of Sam Kinison," *Paul Luvera Journal,* November 30,

2009, www.paulluvera.com/weblog/2009/11/the-strange-death-of
-sam-kinison.

Page 113 *"was dying from end-stage liver cancer"*: Madelaine Lawrence, *The Death View Revolution* (Hove, UK: White Crow Books, 2014), 94.

Page 115 *"a person's fear of death often diminishes"*: C. W. Kerr, J. P. Donnelly, S. T. Wright, S. M. Kuszczak, A. Banas, P. C. Grant, and D. L. Luczkiewicz, "End-of-Life Dreams and Visions: A Longitudinal Study of Hospice Patients' Experiences," *Journal of Palliative Medicine* 17, no. 3 (March 2014): 296.

Page 115 *"Hallucinations and visions"*: "What to Expect When Your Loved One Is Dying," reviewed by Dr. Laura J. Martin, WebMD, July 31, 2016, www.webmd.com/palliative-care/journeys-end-active-dying.

Page 119 *"After years of failed treatments, he agreed"*: Carl Zimmer quoted by Michael Zhang, "The Human Eye Can See in Ultraviolet When the Lens Is Removed," PetaPixel, April 17, 2012, www.petapixel.com /2012/04/17/the-human-eye-can-see-in-ultraviolet-when-the-lens-is -removed.

Chapter Eight: Lullabies and Good-Byes

Page 122 *Of the 800 potential phonemes, the infant*: Patricia K. Kuhl, "Baby Talk," *Scientific American* (November 2015): 64.

Page 123 *parents and infants communicate energetically*: Geoffrey Leigh, Jean Metzker, and Nathan Metzker, "Essence Theory: Reconceptualizing Our View of Children" (unpublished journal article, University of Nevada, 2012), 50.

Page 125 *"It may be our infants who teach us"*: Ibid., 50.

Page 126 *"As my telepathic skills were increasing"*: Terri Daniel, *A Swan in Heaven* (Portland, OR: First House Press, 2008), 1.

Page 128 *humans have an inborn ability to understand shapes*: Jandy Jeppson, with Judith A. Myers-Walls, "Shapes," Purdue University Parent-Provider Partnership, www.extension.purdue.edu/providerparent/child %20growth-development/Shapes.htm, accessed July 10, 2016.

Page 132 *27 percent heard, understood, and responded emotionally*: Madelaine Lawrence, *In a World of Their Own* (Westport, CT: Bergin and Garvey, 1997), 6.

Page 132 *"If anyone asked me, I would swear"*: Ibid., 64.

Page 132 *"It was very strange"*: Ibid., 63.

Page 133 *"Hearing is not the last to go"*: Ibid., 76.

Page 133 *"I also knew there was a love affair"*: Ibid., 42.

Page 133 *"Tell the nurse who said"*: Ibid., 41.

Page 133 *"When the physical body system is compromised"*: Ibid., 154.

Page 139 *normal cognition, or lucidity, does occur*: "Alexander Batthyany-Preliminary Data 2014," July 23, 2015, www.youtube.com/watch?v=Eto AwKSWwsw, accessed May 2016.

Page 140 *"I know from experience that"*: Melinda Ziemer, "End-of-Life Care: The Spirituality of Living When Dying," *Royal College of Psychiatry Newsletter*, www.rcpsych.ac.uk/pdf/Melinda%20Ziemer%20End -of-life%20Care%20the%20Spirituality%20of%20Living%20when %20Dying.pdf, accessed November 17, 2016.

Page 141 *"A statement we heard from people"*: C. W. Kerr, J. P. Donnelly, S. T. Wright, S. M. Kuszczak, A. Banas, P. C. Grant, and D. L. Luczkiewicz, "End-of-Life Dreams and Visions: A Longitudinal Study of Hospice Patients' Experiences," *Journal of Palliative Medicine* 17, no. 3 (March 2014): 296.

Chapter Nine: I'll Call You When I Get There

Page 144 *"The percentage of people reporting contact"*: Julia Assante, *The Last Frontier* (Novato, CA: New World Library, 2012), 53.

Page 149 *"After Duffy's passing"*: Terri Segal, "My Dear Duffy," *Journal for Spiritual and Consciousness Studies* (October 2015): 15.

Page 152 *"Duffy left this world"*: Ibid., 16.

Conclusion: Hearing Is Healing

Page 174 *"transcendental awareness"*: Kenneth Ring and Sharon Cooper, *Mindsight* (Palo Alto, CA: William James Center for Consciousness Studies at the Institute of Transpersonal Psychology, 1999), 163.

Index

disorientation, 89–90

dogs, 112

doorbells, synchronicities involving, 153

Dreaming beyond Death (Bulkeley and Bulkley), 46

dreams, 147; after-death communication through, 147–50; brain during, 50–51; end-of-life, 115; fear/anxiety reduced through, 48; of journeys, 57–58; metaphors and, 50–53; precognitive, 147; research studies on, 58; in shamanic traditions, 51–52; synchronistic, 148; "visitations" in, 148–50

dual realities, 92–93, 94

dying, process of: curiosity about, 103; describing, 27–28; metaphorical evolution during, 48–50

dying, the: breakthroughs experienced by, 14–15; final requests of, 16–18; language of, 31, 39; life of, images reflecting, 172–73; life of, travel metaphors relating to, 55; listening to/honoring, 20–23, 53, 176; metaphorical language of, 41–44; questions asked by, 13–14, 18–20; rapport building with, 18–20, 86–87, 116–17; sitting quietly with, 22; unresolved issues of, 17–18; unspoken connections of, 140–42; visions/dreams of, 58, 116–17; "visitations" experienced by, 15

Eason, Adam, 69

Ebert, Chaz, 10

Ebert, Roger, 10, 14

echolocation, 118, 121

Edison, Thomas, 10, 13, 63

Egyptians, ancient, 51

eight, number, 66, 67

eighteen, number, 161–63

electricity, synchronicities involving, 153–56

Elliott, Kaye, 158–59

Embracing Death (Daniel), 126

"End-of-Life Care" (Ziemer), 140–41

end-of-life language, as metaphorical, 41–44

energy surges, 152–53

enlightenment, 98, 99–100

Erikson, Milton, 98

Espinosa-Jones, Cheryl, 130–31

Esquire magazine, 10

"Essence Theory" (unpublished paper; Leigh, Metzker, and Metzker), 123, 125, 127, 134

evolutionary programming, 117

exclamations of motion, 68–69

exclamations of wonder, 62, 63–64

Experience of a Lifetime, The (North), 64–65

extrasensory experiences, 133–34

Facebook, 2

family, deceased, 15, 32, 39, 95, 107–10. *See also* after-death communication

Famous Last Words, Fond Farewells (Robinson), 10–11

fear, dreams and, 48

figurative language, 4–5, 26, 27

Final Gifts (Callanan and Kelley), 5

final pleasures, 135–36

final requests, 1, 16–18

final words: author's father's, 3–5, 9; cross-linguistic analysis of, 170–71; of death row inmates, 60; of famous

About the Author

L isa Smartt, MA, is a linguist, educator, and poet. She founded
the Final Words Project, an ongoing study devoted to collect-
ing and interpreting the mysterious communications at the end
of life. She cofacilitates workshops on language and consciousness
with Raymond Moody at hospices, universities, and conferences.
She lives in Athens, Georgia, with her husband, John. Learn more
about the Final Words Project at www.finalwordsproject.org or at
www.facebook.com/finalwordsproject.